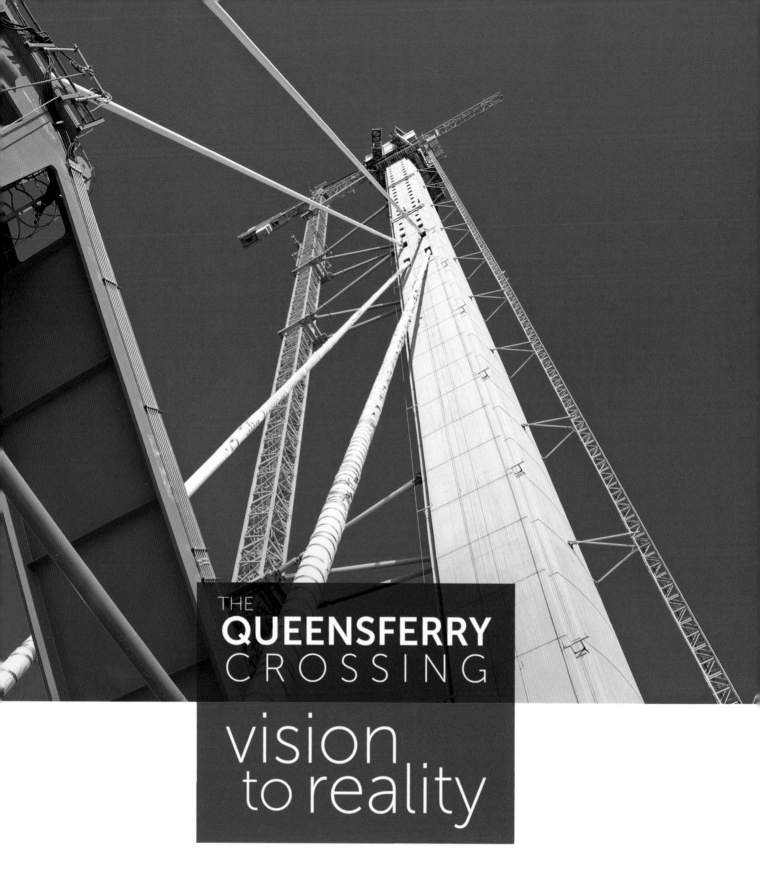

THE QUEENSFERRY CROSSING

vision to reality

Published by: Lily Publications, PO Box 33, Ramsey, Isle of Man IM99 4LP
Tel: +44 (0) 1624 898446   Fax: +44 (0) 1624 898449   E-mail:lilypubs@manx.net   Website:
www.lilypublications.co.uk

This book is dedicated to the men and women

responsible for the design and construction of

the Queensferry Crossing

Researched, written and edited: David Watt

Photo Editor: Derek Chambers

Design: Miles Cowsill and Andrew Lowe

Produced and designed by Lily Publications Ltd
PO Box 33, Ramsey, Isle of Man, British Isles, IM99 4LP
Tel: +44 (0) 1624 898446   Fax: +44 (0) 1624 898449
www.lilypublications.co.uk E-Mail: info@lilypublications.co.uk

Printed and bound by Gomer Press Ltd, Wales, UK +44 (0) 1559 362371 © Lily Publications Ltd 2017

ISBN 978-1-911177-19-7

Contents

Acknowledgements

My sincere thanks go to all members of staff involved in the design and construction of this magnificent new bridge for their endless patience in answering my stream of questions, for providing such clear explanations of the myriad technical operations involved and for their help in capturing the photographs which illuminate the text. A team more capable of successfully meeting the challenges involved in the enormous construction task now completed would be impossible to find.

Particular thanks to:

Derek Chambers, Photo Editor
Miles Cowsill, Lily Publications
Michael Martin
David Climie
Richard Hornby
Mike Glover
Peter Curran
Don Fraser
Lawrence Shackman
Iain Murray
Ewen Macdonell
Keith MacPhail
Colin Goodsir

Photographic Credits

Anna Henly, www.annahenly.com
Tony Gorzkowski, www.whitehousestudios.co.uk
Brian Sutherland, www.flipphotography.co.uk
Paul Baralos, staff
Benn Isherwood, staff
Stephen Knox, staff

Many of the photographs in this book are reproduced courtesy of Transport Scotland.

Photographs of the official opening ceremony courtesy of the Press Association and Unique Events Ltd.

David Watt
September 2017

Rt Hon Nicola Sturgeon MSP, First Minister of Scotland

THE Queensferry Crossing was opened to traffic on 30th August 2017 and officially opened by Her Majesty The Queen on 4th September 2017, the 53rd anniversary of her opening of its neighbour, the Forth Road Bridge.

This unique setting of major bridges from the past three centuries clearly demonstrates how bridge engineering has developed over the years, while the fundamental structural principles remain unaltered. The Queensferry Crossing deck was constructed as three balanced cantilevers in a similar manner to the Forth Bridge in the 1880s. Its two flanking towers are founded on caisson foundations in the Forth again reflecting the supporting structures and methods used on the Forth Bridge.

The Forth Replacement Crossing project has progressed from a concept in 2007 to a finished functioning transport corridor in under ten years and has been funded through the Scottish Government's capital budget.

The bridge protects a vital link in the infrastructure of Scotland forming part of the main north-south artery on the east side of the country from Edinburgh to Fife, Perth,

Dundee and Aberdeen. The added resilience it provides to the trunk road network through the addition of hard shoulders, wind shielding and a 22km long corridor managed with an Intelligent Transport System will bring huge benefits to the Scottish economy.

The Queensferry Crossing has the highest bridge towers in the UK and is the longest three-tower cable-stayed bridge in the world. This magnificent achievement has been made possible by the dedicated site workforce who have worked in the often inhospitable weather conditions of the Firth of Forth. Well over 15,000 workers have spent over 19 million working hours in turning the initial concept design into a steel, concrete and asphalt reality.

The new Queensferry Crossing has generated huge excitement in the local communities on either side of the Forth as it has gradually appeared out of the water and then "spread its wings" to connect the new approach roads on either side.

My congratulations and admiration go to every person who has been involved in this record breaking project.

David Climie
Transport Scotland Project Director

GROWING up in Perth in the 1960s and '70s, a regular highlight was any trip to Edinburgh, driving across the stunning new Forth Road Bridge and admiring the magnificent Forth Bridge from the previous century. The sight fired my passion for civil engineering which led me on to study at Heriot Watt University just a few short miles from these wonderful bridges. Having graduated in 1983 and working for Cleveland Bridge, a world famous structural steelwork company based in North East England, I was thrilled to be appointed as Site Agent on the project to strengthen the Forth Road Bridge tower cross bracings in 1988. I spent the next eighteen months gaining a first-hand appreciation of the challenges of major construction works at height in the exposed conditions of the Firth of Forth.

Having been privileged to go on to work on four long-span suspension bridges around the world, the opportunity arose in 2010 to return home and become Project Director for Transport Scotland on the Forth Replacement Crossing project. It was an easy decision to accept this new challenge with its ambitious timescale to authorise, procure, design and construct the new crossing and its connecting roads. In common, I suspect, with all construction projects, the past seven years have been immensely rewarding and, at times, frustrating and vexing, too. Working in, on and above the Forth has not become any easier over the years.

I am delighted to express my profound admiration and appreciation of the many thousands of individuals who have contributed to this superb project and who, working in close teamwork, have converted it from a vision to a reality in only ten years.

Every one of them will have their own stories to tell of "their road" or "their bridge" and how it wouldn't have been possible without their input. Ultimately, of course, that is true and my personal thanks go to all of them for their dedication, expertise, humour and enthusiasm in delivering a 21st century icon for Scotland.

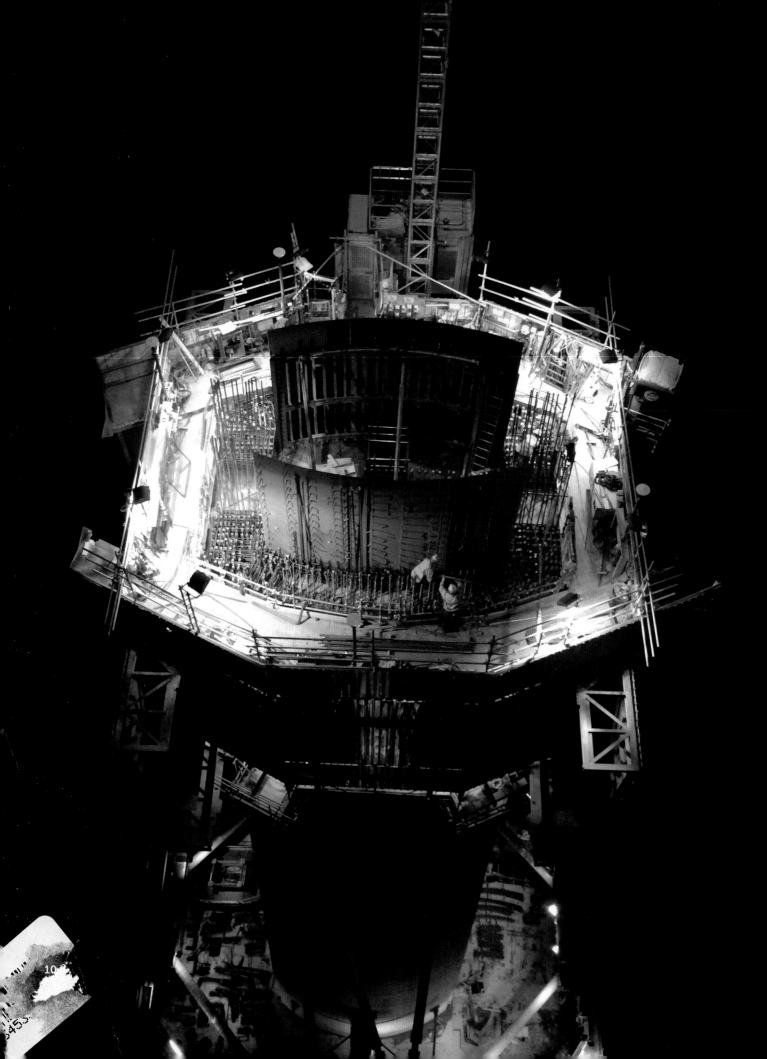

Roy Brannen & Sally Cox
Chairs of Transport Scotland and FCBC Management Boards

F EW structures anywhere in the world more ably reflect the advantages which a partnership approach brings to the successful delivery of a major construction project than the Queensferry Crossing.

At many levels, this wonderful new bridge represents teamwork at its best – between client, contractor and designer, between companies working in joint venture and, of course, between the many thousands of skilled individuals whose expertise and dedication have, over the past six years, created the striking and iconic landmark on the Forth with which we are becoming so familiar.

Throughout the demanding, fast-track and complex construction programme, the various parties involved have maintained a close and positive working relationship at all times, enabling every challenge to be met head on and every obstacle (and, in common with all construction projects the world over, there have naturally been a few) to

be overcome. The quality of the end result speaks for itself and a new global landmark takes its rightful place among the great bridges of the world.

As Chairs of our respective Management Boards overseeing the construction of the Queensferry Crossing, we wish jointly to thank our Board members for their invaluable advice, wisdom and support. Theirs has been an important contribution to the project as a whole.

On behalf of both Boards, we also congratulate and thank everybody involved in the bridge's design and construction on a job magnificently well done. It is a 21st century achievement of which they should be proud, just as the nation is. We all now share the excitement of seeing a new, world-class bridge take its place next to its illustrious and famous neighbours.

We have the utmost admiration for what civil engineering at its finest can achieve.

Client

Scottish Government
Riaghaltas na h-Alba
gov.scot

TRANSPORT
SCOTLAND

Client's advisors

JACOBS ARUP

Principal Contractor & Designers
Forth Crossing Bridge Constructors

FCBC
DRAGADOS | AMERICAN BRIDGE INTERNATIONAL
HOCHTIEF | MORRISON CONSTRUCTION
Queensferry Crossing

HOCHTIEF

DRAGADOS

AB American Bridge INTERNATIONAL

Morrison Construction

Ramboll
Sweco
Leonhardt, Andrä und Partner

ForthCrossingDesignJV

RAMBOLL

SWECO

Leonhardt, Andrä und Partner

Fife ITS	M9 Junction 1A	Contact and Education Centre and Traffic Scotland Control Centre
GRAHAM CONSTRUCTION	SRB Civil Engineering Limited ROADBRIDGE SISK	DAWN
mouchel	RAMBOLL	JACOBS ARUP
RAMBOLL		
AECOM	WSP	

The Challenges
by Michael Martin, FCBC Project Director

N my student days, I was taught that civil engineering is about making life better for people. Today, over forty years later, I still believe that to be true – at least on a macro scale. On a day-to-day basis, however, civil engineering is about something rather less philanthropic. It's about challenges: acknowledging them, assessing them, confronting them and overcoming them.

So it is with any construction project. During my career, I count myself fortunate to have been involved in a wide variety of major infrastructure developments, including several significant bridges. I can attest to the fact that finding solutions to the countless challenges that daily arise is part and parcel of any bridge project. But the Queensferry Crossing is not just 'any bridge project'. It is one of the largest and most complex civil engineering projects of any type undertaken anywhere in the world so far in the 21st century. From beginning to end, it represented a series of enormous challenges which tested the skills of every member of the Project team.

It is people who build bridges. So, the first challenge was how to create a single, coherent, focused team from the many separate organisations involved – a team capable of meeting the challenges head on and lasting the course. FCBC's four international partner companies are all experts in their specialist fields but this was the first time they had worked together in a joint venture. Each had their own distinctive company ethos, cultural background and language (even between Scots and Americans language can be a problem!) In turn, FCBC's designers, the Forth Crossing Design Joint Venture, was a new consortium originally comprising four independent engineering design companies. The client, Transport Scotland, and their advisers were likewise in a 'first time' joint venture. To this mix would be added a large number of major sub-contractors and suppliers from Scotland, the rest of the UK and abroad all making an invaluable contribution.

The objective was for all parties to commit themselves from day one to an agreed strategy and to establish the governance of the Project, its administration, the final design, the construction programme, the construction methods, the safety regime and the high quality demanded by the Contract. In other words, how to make the whole thing come together within a framework of common understanding, common purpose and close teamwork. This first challenge remained a constant companion as the Project progressed through its many phases.

As with most construction projects, the nature of the Queensferry Crossing works constantly changed throughout the life of the Project and the team had to change with it. The earlier years necessarily saw the focus on the construction of the separate elements of the bridge – the foundations, the towers, the road deck, the viaducts and their supporting piers as well as the new approach roads. As the works progressed, these various isolated elements became ever more closely entwined and the technical skills and communications methods within the construction departments had to evolve in order to become focused on the demands of the Project as a single entity. This is the point at which the team needed to migrate from separate groups concentrating on individual challenges to a single team focused on bringing the different parts of the Project together. So, the team had constantly to re-invent and realign itself, moving beyond individual tasks and specific goals so as to be able to tackle the demands of meeting the single, joint goal of finishing

Above: Weather was a constant challenge during construction. Rain, sleet, darkness and the ever present wind all made their presence felt out in the exposed Firth of Forth.

the job successfully and safely, in the process creating a magnificent new world class structure of which we would all be proud.

On a project of this scale, initial resourcing and set-up of the site was always going to be a daunting task. Recruiting several thousand skilled and experienced staff, identifying the best subcontractors, sourcing tens of millions of pounds worth of marine and land plant and other materials from all over the world took many months of detailed planning. Indeed, this was an ongoing task throughout the subsequent six year construction programme since there would be a constant need for new and specialist personnel to come on board as the various phases of construction were completed and new tasks came to the fore. All personnel had to be inducted and introduced to the safety ethos of the Project as well as given an understanding of where they would be working and the importance of the operations they would be expected to undertake. With up to 1,500 people on-site at any one time, these tasks in themselves demanded dedicated health and safety, training and staff induction teams to manage the challenges.

The next challenge was the obvious, logistical one: how to build one of the world's great bridges, carrying 2.7km of four-laned motorway and around 24 million vehicles per year, across one of the most exposed and busy waterways in Europe, the Firth of Forth, without disrupting shipping. On land, a large part of the overall works would have to be built along the line of existing busy trunk and local roads

without delaying traffic unduly. Quite apart from the 'permanent' works - the bridge itself, its foundations, towers, approach viaducts and road deck – and the several kilometres of new connecting trunk road, there were also some of the most complex 'temporary' works ever attempted in the UK. These allowed each element of the permanent works to be built safely and to exacting tolerances. The exposed location, harsh environment, constantly changing tidal conditions and unpredictable weather, especially the almost unrelenting wind, would have a large say in how the works proceeded throughout the lifetime of the Project. Detailed forward programming, close liaison with the Met Office and astute construction techniques, such as off-site pre-fabrication and pre-assembly of components, did much to mitigate the geographical and metereological conditions. Nevertheless, the weather was the one factor which posed constant challenges to the construction programme governing the works.

The Forth is an exceptionally busy marine waterway with all manner of vessels plying their way east and west between the North Sea and the Grangemouth oil refinery and the Port of Rosyth. Not only were we constructing the new bridge high above these busy sea-lanes, but FCBC's marine traffic, heading to and fro between the construction

Above: In the midst of a busy sea-lane, positioning the caissons and placing the foundations were amongst the most challenging operations in the entire construction programme.

site and our base in Rosyth Docks, had to steer directly across the bulk of the traffic. Close liaison with Forth Ports plc was absolutely vital and ensured a successful record of marine safety throughout, a notable achievement.

The construction of any structure does not happen in isolation. Every project is set in its own unique context with regard to the nearby centres of population as well as the local flora and fauna which might be impacted. So the challenge was to carry out every construction task to the very best of our ability while placing care for local residents, the local environment and local wildlife at the top of our priorities. Various liaison groups were established to give a voice to the many parties whose lives would be affected by the Project, creating a valuable forum for two-way communication. At the same time, as is only to be expected with a public sector financed project of this scale, we were working under the scrutiny of the public and a range of commentators and observers who all had their own expectations.

I have always held safety at the very top of my priorities. Happily, the construction industry's safety record has improved enormously in recent years. The safety

performance on the Queensferry Crossing Project, when compared to that achieved by our predecessors on the Forth Road Bridge, demonstrates this – as, in turn, did their performance over *their* predecessors working on the Forth Bridge. But the safety 'race' has no finishing line. Constantly seeking best practice, you are nevertheless only as good as your performance on each given day with fresh challenges appearing with each new dawn. Even in an 'ordinary' company environment, establishing a consistently high safety record is difficult to achieve. On a vast, disparate construction site such as the Queensferry Crossing, with an ever changing, multi-national workforce working in exposed and challenging conditions, often at extreme height, safety becomes an ever present challenge on, I believe, an altogether different scale to almost every other sector of industry. The extent of that challenge was brought home to us in April 2016. Our respected colleague and a friend to many, John Cousin, was tragically killed in an accident on-site which affected us all deeply. While,

overall, our safety performance was good, for me and my colleagues it was not good enough. The loss of a life was the one thing above all else we wished to avoid. Our sadness over John's loss will stay with us, but we realise it pales against that of his family. The 'race' for safety truly has no finishing line; it's a challenge which must continue indefinitely.

The Queensferry Crossing was a 'Design and Construct' contract with the Project's Design Joint Venture employed to work with FCBC to develop the client's specimen design into the final, built structure. I extend my thanks to the designer's team, led by Peter Curran and their on-site staff led by Don Fraser, for their expertise, hard work and dedication. It is inevitable on such a complex, fast track project that many challenges arise as construction proceeds and design considerations alter to reflect progress on-site. This is where the relationship between contractor and designer must be at its strongest, allowing issues to be resolved without impacting on the construction programme. I have known Don for many years, having worked with him on other major bridge projects in Scotland. I knew I could rely on his calm advice and experienced support when the inevitable challenges emerged.

I was equally fortunate to have David Climie as my opposite number heading up the client's delivery team. David is a vastly talented bridge engineer who, unusually for somebody in the client role, has plenty of first-hand experience of sitting in the seat I occupied.

He intuitively understands the daily challenges and frustrations experienced in the imperfect world that is bridge construction and was unfailing in his support and encouragement not only to me but to my entire team. For

that I am very grateful.

I also wish to record my thanks to Sally Cox, Chair of FCBC, and her board members representing our Joint Venture's four partner companies for their invaluable support and help. Thanks, too, go to Alan Platt and David Gough, respectively my Construction and Commercial Directors. Two better 'right hands' would be impossible to find.

For civil engineers, the Queensferry Crossing has been a dream come true. A construction project of this scale and significance likely comes along just once in a career. Overall – and I still find this remarkable – more than 15,000 people from over 30 nationalities with around 20 different languages worked on this wonderful bridge. They came together to combine their knowledge, talents and expertise and formed a single, dedicated, professional team focussed on overcoming the challenges involved in the design and construction of one of the world's great bridges. They were helped by an army of subcontractors, suppliers, consultants and other specialist services. Successfully completing such an enormous 'fast track' project within the client's budget is a tribute to the professionalism of all who were involved at whatever stage and for however long. Without them, the challenges would have remained unmet, the bridge unbuilt.

It has been an honour to have led the construction team. It is my privilege to congratulate them on the magnificent job they have performed. On behalf of this and future generations, my final task on this memorable project is to express my thanks to each and every one of them.

Queensferry Crossing: key facts

2.7km north to south
The world's longest 3 tower cable-stayed bridge

19,000,000 man hours
to complete the 6 year construction programme

210m – Central Tower height
100m taller than the Forth Bridge cantilevers
50m taller than Forth Road Bridge towers
33m taller than London's BT Tower

14m x 16m – towers cross section at bottom
5m x 7.5m at top
Tower wall thickness 1600mm at bottom,
900mm at top

208,000m3 of concrete
or 500,000 tonnes
enough to fill 84 Olympic swimming pools

35,000 tonnes of steel
The equivalent of almost 200 Boeing 747s

37,000km of steel wire
Making 11,000 strands
and 288 stay cables from 94m to 420m long
enough to circle the earth – almost

67,000m2 of road surfacing
Creating 2 motorway lanes and a hard shoulder
in each direction

644m Length of Central Tower span
The longest free-standing, balanced cantilever ever
constructed anywhere in the world

122 deck segments lifted up 60m
to create a road deck
39.8m wide, 16.2m long, 4.5m deep
average 750 tonnes
(with concrete deck pre-installed)

115mph windshielding panels
Keeping the bridge open and bridge users safe
in extreme conditions

CHAPTER 1

Historical Perspective and Background

P ROUD of the country's long tradition of bridge building, people in Scotland took a keen interest in the Forth Replacement Crossing Project from its inception. That's why, when the opportunity arose for members of the public to have a say in what the new bridge would be officially called, over 35,000 people took part in a public ballot which produced the name with which we are now all familiar - a name which is recognised at home and abroad as symbolising one of the world's great bridges.

The Queensferry Crossing is a majestic, 21st century bridge spanning the Firth of Forth. The longest three-tower, cable-stayed bridge in the world, it proudly takes its place alongside those two other engineering marvels of their respective ages: the Victorian wonder that is the Forth Bridge and the similarly revolutionary Forth Road Bridge of the 1960s. Where else in the world can you find three iconic bridges spanning three centuries and representing the highest standards of civil engineering achieved in each?

Forming the centrepiece of the Scottish Government's decade-long Forth Replacement Crossing (FRC) Project, the Queensferry Crossing was the biggest infrastructure development undertaken in Scotland for a generation.

Prompted by significant doubts about the viability of the Forth Road Bridge, in just a little over ten years one of the world's most impressive modern bridges was developed, subjected to extensive public consultation and detailed scrutiny by the Scottish Parliament, procured, constructed and opened to traffic. This book explores many remarkable things about this once in a lifetime project, not least the successful construction and delivery of a bridge of this monumental scale in such a compressed timescale.

The Firth of Forth separates Edinburgh and the Lothians from the Kingdom of Fife to the north. The shortest existing crossings of the Forth at Queensferry, approximately 12km west of Edinburgh, are the two historic, grade A listed bridges – the famous Forth Bridge cantilever rail crossing, completed in 1890 and opened by HRH The Prince of Wales (later King Edward VII), and the Forth Road Bridge, Britain's first long-span suspension crossing which was opened in September 1964 by Her Majesty The Queen.

The Forth Road Bridge has successfully carried road traffic across the Firth of Forth ever since. However, the deteriorating condition of the bridge, particularly corrosion in the main suspension cables and the recognition of the

Opposite page and this page: **The construction of the Forth Road Bridge, opened by Her Majesty The Queen on 4th September 1964, was a technological triumph of its day, transforming road communications in the east of Scotland. The Queen returned in September 2014 to join in the bridge's 50th anniversary celebrations.**

Above: Aerial view of the Firth of Forth from the south before construction of the Queensferry Crossing began.

Opposite page top: An early multi-modal design proposal allowing for a light railway and pedestrian access assuming no future use for the Forth Road Bridge.

huge, long term disruption that rehabilitation measures would unavoidably cause, resulted in the need for a replacement crossing to secure the future of cross-Forth travel. At the start of its life, the Forth Road Bridge carried around four million vehicles per year, providing a vital commercial and social link between Fife, Edinburgh and the north and east of Scotland. Half a century later, it was carrying around 24 million vehicles per year, by any standards a dramatic increase and one which inevitably brought significant wear and tear.

The exposure to risk represented by this deterioration was graphically brought home in December 2015 when a truss end-link failed. The emergency repair works required the bridge to be entirely closed to all traffic for three weeks and caused severe disruption on both sides of the Forth and for many miles around. By that time, of course, its new neighbour, the Queensferry Crossing, was well under construction, but the closure amply demonstrated the problems that would be faced had a "do nothing" strategy prevailed. Furthermore, the Forth Road Bridge's lack of hard

shoulders and protection against wind have also shown up its lack of resilience over the years, closures and restrictions having become regular features. As the ever increasing use and, therefore, the economic and strategic importance of the bridge grew year on year, so the need for a more reliable replacement became ever clearer.

Following inspection of the main Forth Road Bridge suspension cables in 2005, a significant number of broken or corroded internal wires were identified resulting in an estimated loss of around 8% of their total strength. This led to a dramatic prediction of complete closure as early as 2018. A subsequent cable inspection in 2008 indicated the cables may have been deteriorating at a slower rate than the most pessimistic estimate, although the strength loss was re-assessed to be around 10%. This led to a revised estimate of 2017 to 2021 before any traffic restrictions could be required. The Forth Estuary Transport Authority (FETA), the bridge operating authority at the time, implemented dehumidification of the west suspension cable in 2008 and the east cable in 2009. Further inspections indicated a reduction in the corrosion rate of the cables but it remained the case that no unconditional guarantees could be made about their future viability and, as had already been established, a significant percentage of their strength had already gone. Closing the bridge to HGVs

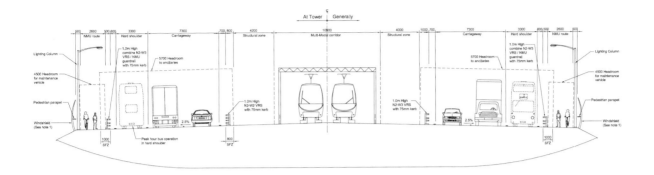

and potentially other classes of vehicles would have had a very serious negative economic impact. These facts, together with other significant on-going maintenance issues, led the Scottish Government to conclude that the Forth Road Bridge could not continue as the main crossing for all traffic. It was – or would shortly become – no longer fit for purpose.

Following the initial cable investigations, in 2006 Transport Scotland commissioned the "Forth Replacement Crossing Study" to determine the best solution. This used the Scottish Transport Appraisal Guidance (STAG)

methodology which is an evidence-led, objective-based appraisal process. Eight transport planning objectives were established at an early stage, based around:

- capacity
- accessibility
- environment
- maintainability
- connectivity
- reliability
- increasing travel choices and
- sustainable development

Above: A computer generated image looking south-west showing how this unique location for bridges would look once the Queensferry Crossing was completed.

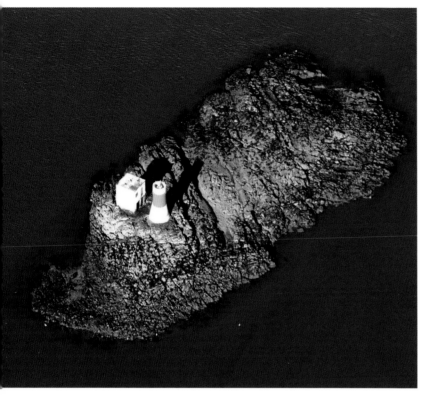

Above: Situated in mid estuary, the Beamer Rock made an ideal location for the Central Tower's foundations. Its famous navigational light was dismantled and stored ready for rebuilding on nearby land in the future.

A key objective of the study was that traffic capacity should generally remain at 2006 levels and any replacement crossing should not result in a marked increase in cross-Forth traffic volume.

The location is particularly environmentally sensitive. Detailed reviews of the local area were required due to the existence of European designated protected habitats for rare and migratory birds, conservation areas with listed species of flora and fauna, wetlands of international importance (including UNESCO "Ramsar" sites) and areas of national importance for wildlife or geology (Sites of Special Scientific Interest).

No fewer than 65 options were initially sifted, including tunnels, bridges and barrages, along with five potential routes – or corridors – for the new crossing. Following progressively detailed appraisals of bridges and tunnels in the most suitable corridors, a cable-stayed bridge in corridor 'D', immediately to the west of the Forth Road Bridge, was recommended as the preferred scheme. This alignment makes use of Beamer Rock, a natural dolerite outcrop in the middle of the Forth, providing a suitably strong and effective location for the proposed bridge's central tower foundation. It was the natural choice.

Following a comprehensive public consultation exercise in mid-2007 and further consideration of the means to accommodate future travel demands across the Forth, it was initially determined that the replacement crossing should be 'multi-modal'. This meant that the new bridge would be wider than previously envisaged, at around 50m and would include designated facilities for guided buses or a light-rail system. Pedestrians and cyclists would also be accommodated on dedicated lanes, located at the edges of the structure.

This recommendation was accepted by Scottish Ministers and announced by John Swinney MSP, Cabinet Secretary for Finance and Sustainable Growth, in December 2007. The estimated cost was to be between £3.2 billion and £4.2 billion and it would be delivered by the end of 2016, just ahead of expected traffic restrictions on the Forth Road Bridge. Chapter Two looks at how Transport Scotland developed and refined the plans until the stage was reached when tenders could be invited from potential constructors.

FORTH BRIDGE

Constructed:	1883 – 1890
Cost:	£3.2m
Design:	Cantilever rail bridge
Designed by:	Sir John Fowler and Sir Benjamin Baker
Contractor:	Tancred Arrol
Length:	2.5km (1.5 miles)
Tower height:	100m (330ft) above mean water level
Quantity of steel:	65,000 tonnes
No. of rivets:	6.5 million (The last rivet was inserted by HRH The Prince of Wales, later King Edward VII)
Myth:	Contrary to popular belief, painting the bridge was never continuous. However, a maintenance crew is permanently active on-site
Paint:	It takes over 200,000 litres of paint to cover the bridge's 145 acres of surface. The long-life polymer coating applied in 2011 will last 25 years
Names:	The 3 famous double cantilevers have names: Queensferry, Inchgarvie and Fife

FORTH ROAD BRIDGE

Constructed:	1958 – 1964
Cost:	£19.5m
Design:	Suspension road bridge
Designed by:	Mott, Hay & Anderson and Freeman Fox & Partners
Consultant architect:	Sir Giles Gilbert Scott, designer of the world famous British telephone kiosk
Contractor:	Arrol, Cleveland, Dorman Long (ACD)
Central span:	1,006m (3,320ft) longest in Europe at the time
Length:	2.5km (1.5 miles)
Tower height:	150m (495ft) above mean water level
Quantity of steel:	39,600 tonnes
Volume of concrete:	125,000 cubic metres
Quantity of wire:	6,350 tonnes or 30,000 miles – enough to stretch 1.25 times round the world
Traffic:	Each year, almost 24 million vehicles cross the bridge. Statistics show that, typically 2% more vehicles head south than north

CHAPTER 2
Development and Procurement

N early 2008, with the Forth Replacement Crossing Project having been given the green light by Scottish Ministers, Transport Scotland undertook a competitive procurement process culminating in the appointment of a joint venture between Jacobs and Arup, two renowned consulting engineering companies, to support the management and delivery of what everyone now realised would be the biggest Scottish infrastructure project in a generation. This formed an integrated team with Transport Scotland which became known as the Employer's Delivery Team (EDT).

The early prognosis for the Forth Road Bridge had predicted possible restrictions to HGV traffic as early as 2014 with closure to all vehicles by 2018. A replacement crossing was urgently required and time was of the essence. The need for a new crossing was questioned by some members of the public, with suggestions coming forward that, if it went ahead at all, it should be a tunnel and not a bridge. It was clear that robust and informative consultation with local communities was going to be a key consideration in bringing the Project to fruition. It was

initially assumed that the replacement crossing would provide for all road vehicles, public transport, pedestrians and cyclists. No future functional use of the Forth Road Bridge was envisaged. Motorway standard approach road connections were to be provided principally to join the A90/M90 to the north of the Forth and the M9 and A90 to the south, amounting to a total length of 22km.

Initial design development considered a wide range of deck configurations and tower geometries that could accommodate the client's brief. The major constraint on the bridge arrangement was the need to provide for a dedicated public transport corridor across, and beyond, the new bridge, which would have the potential to be converted in the future to a light rapid transit (LRT) system.

Cost

Despite intensive design development and extensive environmental and ground surveys, the very significant cost of the Project was a dominant concern. Although several forms of funding were explored, it was assumed that some

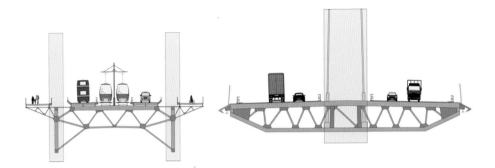

form of public/private partnership would have to be adopted. However, the meltdown of the global financial sector in 2007/8 meant that the Project - at the then forecast cost of £3.2 to £4.2 billion - appeared to be unaffordable.

In response, the EDT embarked on a thorough re-appraisal of the Project scope. By the autumn of 2008, this study had concluded that substantial cost reductions could be achieved by:

- using the existing road infrastructure as much as possible by widening and upgrading it
- introducing Intelligent Transport Systems (ITS) to better manage traffic demand and
- taking on board innovative design solutions for the new bridge, principally by adopting central crossing cables in the two main spans to enable simple, easily maintainable box forms to be used for the deck and towers

To achieve additional value for money, further studies on the potential continuing use of the Forth Road Bridge were undertaken. This followed on from the second cable investigation, as reported by FETA in early 2008, which gave an improved prognosis for the rate of main cable deterioration. Together with the removal of general traffic from the Forth Road Bridge, constituting some 15% of the

Above: Cross section diagrams showing the "Managed Crossing Strategy" using the Forth Road Bridge for public transport on the left and general traffic using the new Queensferry Crossing on the right.

Below: Various forms of tower design can be used on cable-stayed bridges. Ultimately, single slender towers in the middle of the road deck were chosen with parallel stay cable arrays fanning outwards along the centre line of the bridge.

loading in the cables, these factors provided the welcome hope that the existing bridge could, after all, have an important role to play long into the future.

Analysis demonstrated that the residual strength of the weakened Forth Road Bridge was sufficient to provide a dedicated public transport, cycling and pedestrian corridor, with the potential opportunity for a light rapid transit system in the longer term. By removing these functions from the replacement crossing, the design of the new bridge could become significantly narrower, reducing the original 50m width to 40m. Additionally, design development resulted in a thinner deck and a simple mono-tower geometry with the cable arrays aligned along the centre-line of the bridge.

The combination of these measures reduced the estimated cost range for the overall Project to between

Above: An early computer generated image of the completed bridge viewed from the south-west.

Below: A technical drawing showing the position of the new bridge's foundations on the seabed and north and south shores.

£1.73 billion and £2.34 billion. Importantly, this represented a cost level at which the Scottish Government could finance the Project from its own resources. The strategy of combining the two road bridges into a Managed Crossing Strategy was announced in December 2008 and formed the basis for taking the Project forward. Further enhancements to the proposed scheme were developed,

the key aims being to ensure journey time reliability and to enhance public transport services and facilities as far as possible, including dedicated bus lanes within the hard-shoulder in two southbound locations (the first such schemes in Scotland) and an additional 1000 space Park & Ride facility at Halbeath, in partnership with Fife Council.

Statutory Approvals

The initial assumption was that the statutory approvals for the Project would be gained through Road Orders made under the powers of the Roads Scotland Act, with land acquired using the Compulsory Purchase Order

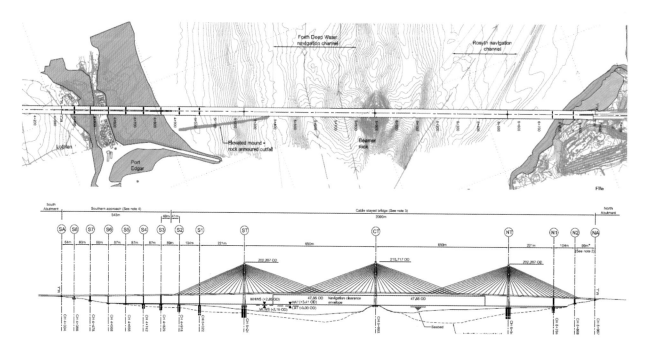

Above: **Members of the Employer's Delivery Team pose for a group photograph in May 2017.**

process. On further consideration, this and other forms of legislation, such as the Transport and Works Act, were deemed to be inappropriate. Thus the non-typical route of raising a Parliamentary Bill was selected, with the distinct advantage of providing a high degree of time certainty. On a project of this scale, however, the level of detail required, the amount of documentation to be produced and the necessary scrutiny of the process were much greater than normal. In the case of the Forth Replacement Crossing, where timing was of the essence, this additional effort was further complicated since the Bill process would have to run in parallel with the lengthy contractor procurement process.

The Forth Crossing Bill was introduced into the Scottish Parliament in November 2009, the same month as the formal tender procurement process commenced, one of the biggest the Scottish Government had ever undertaken.

Following Parliamentary scrutiny throughout the course of 2010, the Forth Crossing Act was passed by 108 votes to 3 votes and granted Royal Assent in January 2011.

Consultation

From its inception, community engagement and communication were built into the heart of the Project. Consultation began in 2006 to inform local communities and a wide range of interested organisations of the Forth Replacement Crossing Study and continued in 2007 to focus on the Study's findings. A sustained programme of engagement with dozens of organisations and thousands of individuals was undertaken throughout 2008 and 2009. These activities gave local communities the opportunity to provide feedback on new developments in the planning stages and made sure that local voices were listened to before important decisions were taken. There were five separate rounds of stakeholder and community briefings and two rounds of public exhibitions in 12 locations across Edinburgh, Fife and West Lothian. The supply of information was on an unprecedented scale for an infrastructure project in Scotland, with a total of 21 community information points, the publication of digital and printed newsletters and extensive coverage in the local and national media.

Contractor Procurement

On a project of such international significance, a programme of close dialogue with the construction industry was essential from the outset to market test the various potential procurement routes and understand the nature of the risks perceived by contractors and how they could be mitigated. This process culminated in the

Above: **Progress review meetings were a prominent feature of daily life.**

selection of two large, international joint venture contractors, comprising some of the best known names in international civil engineering, being invited to tender for the construction of the bridge and its approach roads. Three adjacent road infrastructure and building contracts provided further opportunities for smaller contractors.

Traditional forms of contract were not thought to give the levels of cost and time certainty demanded by this Project. Consequently, the internationally recognized "FIDIC" Silver Book contractual model, established by the International Federation of Consulting Engineers, was adopted because it was simple in its form and, importantly, provided clarity on the apportionment of risk between the parties for the duration of the Project.

Risk Mitigation

In response to the feedback received from the construction industry and in anticipation of the tenderers' concerns about costs and risks, the EDT embarked on a comprehensive programme of surveys, investigations and research, the results of which were made available to the tenderers. Information included:

- the results of tests and analyses demonstrating the behaviour of the crossing cable arrangement
- the definition of the windshield arrangement on the bridge
- the definition of ship impact loading for each element of the structure
- the results of three extensive land and marine ground investigations

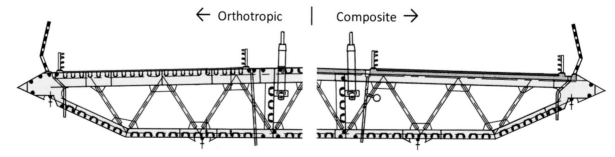

← Orthotropic | Composite →

Above: **Two options were considered for the deck structure: orthotropic (all steel, similar to the Forth Road Bridge) and composite (steel and concrete) which was chosen.**

- the results of wind tunnel testing
- the results of various environmental surveys and
- the relieving of the contractor from the potentially large inflation risk always inherent in contracts of such long duration

In addition, a very detailed land-based design for the network road connections was produced for the tenderers' consideration as well as a specimen design illustrating the potential structural form and materials of the bridge itself, together with a likely construction sequence and programme. The intention was to give the tendering companies as much information as possible to enable them to assess risks, logistics and cost at an early stage of the tender process. The information provided included:

- design options for the bridge, including dimensions and engineering details for the deck, towers and abutments
- options for the main deck, including an orthotropic deck and a composite deck (the latter being selected by the successful tenderer, FCBC)
- options for the approach viaducts, including a concrete and a composite deck (the latter being selected by the successful tenderer)

The specimen design allowed the Project to be crystalised into firm, achievable requirements and laid out an engineering and architectural vision for the new bridge befitting its unique setting beside the neighbouring landmark bridges from the previous two centuries.

Above: **The design study for the shape of the towers considered a solution similar to the Rio Antirrio Bridge in Greece.**

Below: **Various design solutions exist to the challenge of stabilising the towers. From top: additional piers beneath the bridge containing tie-down cables; cables connecting the tower tops; extra long cables attached to each tower top; mid-span cross-over stay cables (chosen for the Queensferry Crossing).**

Specimen Design for the Bridge

The Forth Replacement Crossing Study recommended a three-tower cable-stayed bridge along the chosen alignment slightly to the west of the existing bridges, with main spans of 650m and the central tower founded on

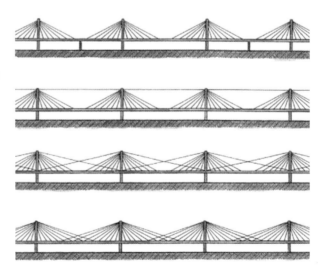

Beamer Rock. The instability of the middle tower of any three-tower cable-stayed bridge is a well-known phenomenon and there are a number of ways of mitigating the instability.

The design recommended by the FRC Study was based on stiff pyramid shaped towers as had been used on the Rio Antirrio Bridge in Greece. An alternative solution was to stabilise the central tower by using two stabilising cables connecting the top of the tower with the intersection of the flanking towers in the deck, as was done for the Ting Kau Bridge in Hong Kong.

The Rio Antirrio solution would have meant visually heavy towers which, it was felt, would have dominated the two existing bridges. The foundation pad of the central tower would also have been too deep and wide to fit the

Above: By mid 2015, tower construction is progressing well with initial road deck sections in place and, from the land, the Approach Viaduct South half way through its launch out over the water.

Beamer Rock outcrop and its construction would have been relatively difficult and expensive.

The Ting Kau solution would have meant very long stabilising cables with large diameters and would have been an inelegant solution both visually and in engineering terms.

The crossed cables design was an ideal engineering solution featuring a slim central tower of exactly the same shape as its flanking towers, with the whole composition not dominating the cantilevers of the Forth Bridge or the towers of the Forth Road Bridge. Moreover, the foundation

of the central tower would be shallow and smaller enabling not only an economic design but one suitable for the Beamer Rock location.

The crossed cable solution had only been used once before - in 1996 for the Rennes Viaduct in France - but never on the scale of the new bridge envisaged for the Forth. However, the merits of this solution were clear and led to it being adopted. The tenderers were invited to submit their bids on the basis of a crossed cable design.

General Arrangement

The total length of the bridge is a little short of 2.7km (2.64km to be precise). Although the bridge was divided into a cable-stayed bridge with southern and northern approach viaducts, the structure was to be continuous from abutment to abutment with no intermediate expansion joints, thus removing the sectional bumps for which the Forth Road Bridge has become renowned.

Above: The view from the crew boat as it arrives at the Central Tower in October 2015 with the road deck beginning to emerge and the Tower - and tower crane - reaching ever higher.

The slender towers were to be vertical, reinforced concrete structures tapering with height and located in the middle of the road deck with two parallel planes of stay cables anchored centrally in the "shadow" of the towers. The deck itself was to be a streamlined box girder of either orthotropic or composite construction.

Considering the centrally anchored stay cables, studies were carried out to investigate the torsional behaviour of the deck under a number of different traffic scenarios to establish appropriate design criteria for the twist of the deck and to confirm that the design met certain requirements.

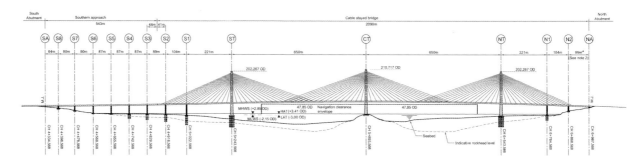

Above: Longitudinal section drawing of the specimen design issued for tender.

Below: The Ting Kau Bridge in Hong Kong showing the long Centre Tower stabilising cables.

Tender Process

A competitive dialogue process was adopted for the tender. This enabled in-depth, confidential discussions with each tenderer regarding the various design and construction issues and the perceived risks associated with the development of the specimen design. It was recognized that this intensive and lengthy process would be more expensive than traditional tender processes, but the benefit to the client in greater clarity in scope and risk mitigation was such that Parliament agreed to reimburse the losing tenderer up to 50% of incurred costs.

The Principal Contract to design and build the new bridge and connecting roads was awarded in April 2011 to the Forth Crossing Bridge Constructors (FCBC) consortium with a successful tender price of £790 million, significantly below the original estimated price range of £900 - £1.2 billion. The improved prognosis for the Forth Road Bridge cables enabled a completion date for the Principal Contract of summer 2017 to be agreed with the successful contractor.

The separate contract to install the Project's Intelligent Transportation System (ITS) on the M90 in Fife, north of the new bridge, was awarded in June 2011 to John Graham (Dromore) Ltd for £12.9 million. On the south side, the separate contract to upgrade Junction 1a of the M9 motorway at Kirkliston was awarded in July 2011 to a consortium between John Sisk and Roadbridge for £25.6 million. The contract to build a Community and Education Centre was awarded in September 2011 to Dawn Construction. All contracts were awarded below the estimated price range.

At the end of the tender process, the projected outturn cost was reviewed to reflect the contract prices, the conditions agreed and the consequent risk reduction. The cost range was £1.45 billion to £1.6 billion - marking a reduction of some £300 million in the procurement process and £2 billion since the outset of the Project.

CHAPTER 3

The Design

L IKE its illustrious neighbours, the Queensferry Crossing represents the very latest in bridge design and engineering of its time. Its unique form makes it one of the most striking architectural structures of the 21st century and a globally important feat of engineering. It is certainly a very fitting addition to one of the most distinctive and famous bridge vistas in the world.

For engineering designers, there is no more rewarding challenge than to be charged with the design of such a monumental structure. On this occasion, that meant embracing the architectural and engineering vision contained in the client's Specimen Design of slender towers and crossing cables. This task was handed to the Forth Crossing Design Joint Venture appointed by main contractor, FCBC, to be their design partner through the tender stage and the entire construction programme. Along the way, many improvements and refinements were incorporated and a constant balance struck between maintaining the design ethos of the bridge and achieving the required quality while ensuring the end product could be built at a reasonable cost.

That, in essence, was the engineering design role played

by the partner companies in the Forth Crossing Design JV, Ramboll, SWECO and Leonhardt Andrä & Partners. The Design JV's detailed design work was undertaken across four centres - Copenhagen, Southampton, Stuttgart and Edinburgh - and brought together 150 experienced designers who translated the design into more than 1,200 technical drawings and documents and a further 20,000 production drawings. Involved in many bridge designs around the world, there was nevertheless a special pride amongst this international team to be working on the design and construction of what everyone knew from the start would become one of the most famous bridges in the world.

This chapter covers the principal design challenges and solutions involved in constructing the Queensferry Crossing. Later chapters look in detail at the actual construction processes used to turn the design vision into reality.

Overview

The Queensferry Crossing has already earned its place among the most notable bridge structures ever built. It is the UK's tallest bridge and the world's longest three-tower cable-stayed bridge. It boasts a unique stay cable form which allows for a slender and elegant tower and deck design. Its technical features and innovative engineering solutions have produced a striking and graceful design that adds to the character and personality of the area while leaving a lasting legacy for the community that it serves and for future generations.

The scale of the structure is awe-inspiring. It is 2.7km long with two main spans each of 650m, two side spans of 223m, 10 approach spans varying from 64m to 104m and three towers that reach between 202m and 210m in height, a considerable 38% higher than the towers of the Forth Road Bridge next door. The cable arrangement of overlapping stay cables at mid-span, specified by the client, represents a design innovation that provides the necessary stiffness to the structural system to enable the towers to be more slender and the deck lighter than would otherwise have been the case.

Comparing the new crossing to the existing Forth Bridges, its design clearly demonstrates how bridge structures have evolved over the years, with modern bridges becoming lighter and stronger. The slim, balanced and harmonious geometric proportions of the Queensferry Crossing's approach spans and the visual continuity between them and the main spans result in a simplicity and elegance of form which does not dominate or detract from the existing bridges in this globally important location for significant bridges. On the contrary, commentators agree that this 21st century addition to the scene adds to the unique aura created by the 19th century Forth Bridge and 20th century Forth Road Bridge. Furthermore, its three towers and striking cable fans complement the design of the world famous Forth Bridge, a UNESCO World Heritage Site since 2015.

Stay Cable Design

Central to the Queensferry Crossing's aesthetic and structural elegance are the highly visible, glistening white cables which cross over at mid-point along the two main spans creating a diamond pattern along a 140m length of the deck. These are often referred to as the bridge's signature design feature. Certainly, they are the most obvious feature which attracts the eye on first seeing the bridge whether from near or far.

In total, there are 288 stay cables each comprising of between 45 and 109 strands made of seven high tensile steel wires 5.2mm in diameter. The cables vary in length from 94m to 420m.

In a fan-like arrangement, the cables spread outwards and downwards from the three towers and overlap at mid-span, making the Queensferry Crossing not only the longest three-tower cable-stayed bridge in the world

Above: Unique amongst major bridges, the Queensferry Crossing's stay cables cross mid span, providing stability for the Central Tower.

but also by far the largest to feature cables which cross at mid-span.

Central Tower

With the two main spans situated above busy, strategic navigation channels in the Firth of Forth, a major challenge to the three-tower design was the stability of the Central Tower.

The critical question was how to stabilise the Central Tower and combine it with as light a road deck as possible while achieving the required overall stiffness of the entire structural system. The solution to this question was reached by extending the spread of the stay cable fans beyond mid-span so that they overlap in the middle region of each span. Supporting this central length of deck with the extra cables results in an increase in the effective stiffness of the overall structure by creating overlapping truss actions. This provides the necessary stability for the Central Tower.

The overlapping stay cables in each of the two main spans double the number of cable supports – from two to four - for each of the ten mid-span deck sections both sides of the Central Tower. As the vertical load is thus shared by multiple cables, the force per cable is relatively low.

This innovative solution to the structural challenge of stabilising the central, mid-estuary tower created a virtual truss system involving a total of 37,000km of wire inside the cables cumulatively stretched between the towers. Adopting this novel solution enabled the Central Tower to be as slim as possible, resulting in all three towers possessing an identical profile tapering with height to a

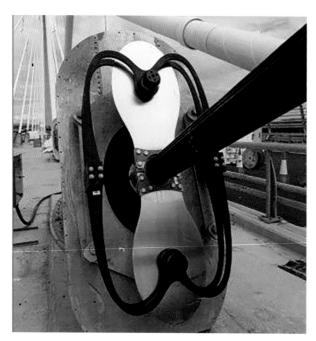

Above: **Dampers at road deck level reduce stay cable vibration and oscillation in windy conditions.**

Above: **The Design team met daily to review progress on-site.**

narrow top. Crucially, this protected the desired light and elegant nature of the bridge's visual impact.

Anchored at top and bottom (high up in the tower structure and, down below, in each deck section respectively), the cables are sheathed in white High Density Polyethylene (HDPE) pipes to provide protection from the elements and prevent corrosion. The pipes feature an external, spiral rib running down their entire length which helps minimise any resonance due to wind induced vibrations.

The cable-stayed design of the bridge makes long term maintenance much more straightforward by allowing individual strands inside the cables to be taken out and replaced without compromising the integrity of the bridge or adversely affecting traffic flows across it.

Road Deck

The overall width of the road deck is 39.8m. It is configured as a three-corridor arrangement with the towers and stay cables located in the central zone between the two carriageways rather than at the edges of the structure. The bridge deck carries two general lanes of motorway traffic in each direction and widened hard shoulders to ensure that breakdowns, incidents and any maintenance works do not cause congestion. The hard shoulders also provide the flexibility to carry buses, perhaps displaced from the Forth Road Bridge during periods of high wind, as well as other forms of public transport should it be required in the future.

The road surface is continuous from abutment to abutment with no joints as it passes over the supporting pier structures or as it passes the three towers. This delivers a smoother driving experience and means there is only the need for four large expansion joints, one each at both ends of the two carriageways, which minimises the number of major components needing regular inspection and maintenance.

The deck design was perfected using software that calculates loading in all areas of the bridge. Computer models were created in the design centre to analyse the whole bridge both during construction and in its final, completed state. Additionally, a series of three dimensional models were used with load cases applied to the model to simulate the self-weight of the bridge as well as various traffic loadings and climatic conditions such as temperature fluctuations and the ever present wind.

A total of 1,300 construction phases were identified and analysed for the erection of the main spans which saw the deck sections being aligned, bolted together with temporary clamps and then welded into position. This modelling was used to monitor and control the geometry of the structure as it was being built with real time survey information being fed into the model to control the alignment and ensure proper fit of the individual deck cantilevers.

The cable-stayed deck is formed of 122 composite steel and concrete sections, comprising 110 standard sections and 12 "starter" sections fixed in position around the three towers. A further 12 sections were integrated into the southern end of the northern approach viaduct structure prior to its launch out into position from land.

The Forth Estuary is renowned for high winds and difficult tides, two critical factors that had to be borne in mind by the design team. Erecting the deck in such a

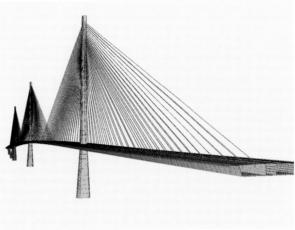

Left: **August 2017: the finished road deck ready to receive traffic for the first time.**

Above: **Modern computer programmes played an important role in predicting how the bridge would behave in certain loading conditions.**

Below: **Progress on deck erection in mid 2016.**

location meant loading conditions during construction would be extreme. The most appropriate erection procedure was, therefore, the balanced cantilever technique which is fully described in Chapter 5.

The road deck super-structure is vertically supported from above by the stay cables and, from below, by the approach viaduct piers and abutments at both ends. It is also supported by being directly attached to the Central Tower via a "power joint", the only point along the entire length of the road deck where it is directly attached to a tower. The deck is not directly connected to the North and South Towers but is free to move longitudinally to allow for its expansion and contraction due to temperature and traffic load fluctuations. However, the deck is supported

laterally at the North and South Towers by bearings which accommodate lateral loads, predominantly wind.

Towers

To create a strong sense of visual quality and beauty to complement the distinctive characteristics of the neighbouring two bridges, the design of the Queensferry Crossing had to deliver slim towers. It is no coincidence that the new bridge's three towers mirror and complement both the three massive, steel-trussed cantilever support towers of the Forth Bridge and the slender towers of the Forth Road Bridge.

In terms of scale, at 202m to 210m Above Ordnance Datum (AOD), the three towers are the tallest of any UK

Above: **Inside the Central Tower's cofferdam on Beamer Rock, prior to concrete foundations being poured.**

bridge. The top of the towers are 147m above deck level, which is up to 50m higher than the main towers of the Forth Road Bridge.

The towers are slim and hollow and are formed from reinforced concrete. The outer dimensions of all three towers are the same, measuring 14m by 16m at their base and tapering gracefully to 5.0m by 7.5m at their pinnacle. The wall thickness of the towers varies from 1.6m to 0.9m as they rise.

Foundations

In order to refine the design of the foundations, engineers and geologists conducted detailed field mapping of the geology of the seabed and carried out detailed inspections of rock cores recovered from below the seabed. From this work, it was possible to identify the quality of rock across the Firth of Forth and to produce a consistent approach for the design of the foundations. All the foundations bear on the top of the rock which eliminates the need for expensive and time-consuming drilling or driving of piles and reduces the risk of delays and cost overruns that can be incurred if localised variations to ground conditions are discovered. Mass concrete foundation solutions were adopted with the method of construction varying according to the conditions at each foundation position. The method selected was influenced by the depth of water, the depth and condition of seabed

soil overlying the rock and the magnitude of load to be imposed by the bridge structure.

The Forth Estuary has varied geology influenced by the same volcanic activity that resulted in the formation of the famous hill Arthur's Seat in the middle of Edinburgh. This is characterised by intrusions of molten rock through the sedimentary, glacial and alluvial deposits. This is particularly notable at the base of the Central Tower which is founded on one such intrusion of dolerite rock known as Beamer Rock, strong and substantial enough to provide a suitable foundation to support the 210m high tower.

The client's Specimen Design called for the towers to rise straight out of the sea rather than have obvious foundations or other protective installations at their bases such as feature on the Forth Road Bridge. At low tide, the top of Beamer Rock on which the Central Tower stands becomes visible. Steel caissons for the North and South Towers and Pier S1 on the southern approach viaduct, sunk into the seabed and filled with concrete, were chosen as the most effective method of creating foundations strong and stable enough to support the weight and height of the towers and piers rising above them. Chapter 4 looks in detail at the construction of the caissons and how they were lowered into position.

The approach adopted of careful investigation, thorough analysis and effective verification of the rock formations during construction ensured the foundations met the

Above: **The south abutment nears completion, proudly displaying the bridge's date plaque.**

stringent design requirements set by the client. The geological information gathered prior to construction was translated into 3D numerical models to inform the design of the foundations. Each foundation excavation was rigorously inspected with a remotely operated camera developed to carry out detailed underwater inspections up to 50m below sea level. Using the geological and engineering expertise of the designer and contractor enabled the delivery of a complex set of foundations in a safe and efficient manner.

Approach Viaducts

The topography of the land and seabed on both sides of the estuary meant that the design of the bridge had to factor in the need for the southern and northern approach viaducts to be launched out from land to overcome the geographical issues associated with restricted access due to steep terrain and shallow water. The launch operations of these two enormous structures presented a series of construction challenges which are described in Chapter 5.

The approach viaduct deck spans on both sides are supported on a series of V-shaped, hollow, reinforced concrete piers varying in height from 10.1m to 49.4m on the southern approach spans and 24.2m to 46.5m on the northern approach spans. Visual aesthetic continuity was maintained by ensuring the inclination of each pier leg was identical, each leg also tapering uniformly with height and

being similar in their finish to the main towers.

From the outset, an important design criterion, happily achieved, was the homogeneity of the three towers and the ten viaduct piers.

Abutments

Descriptions of bridges often overlook the abutment structures at both ends perhaps because, being situated half buried into the land beneath the road deck, they are largely hidden from view and rarely seen by anybody. In fact, abutments are vitally important elements in the overall design and functioning of a bridge, providing the supports at each end and forming the vital transition interface between the bridge spans, the road deck and the land. These two-storey, reinforced concrete structures fulfil several other functions including housing the electrical, mechanical and structural health monitoring equipment and the emergency electrical back-ups essential for the day-to-day management and operation of the bridge.

Windshielding

Windshielding along the length of the deck was another critical consideration to be included in the design and construction of the bridge to ensure that the frequent periods of speed restrictions and closures experienced over the years on the Forth Road Bridge would not be a fact of life on the Queensferry Crossing.

Above: Windshielding panels run along the entire length of the road deck...

Below: ... and are also used in the centre of the bridge either side of the towers to minimise buffeting effects on traffic.

An important factor in the windshield design was to ensure that bridge users could enjoy the views of the estuary as they crossed over, just as they have always done on the Forth Road Bridge. This led to the selection of a design of windshielding with a high degree of transparency. The solution resulted in 3.6m high, open louvre panels being installed which shield vehicles from winds with speeds of up to 115mph whilst simultaneously providing good visibility. Combining modern design with functionality, the windshields have lent great resilience to the bridge, making the crossing much less susceptible to closures during high winds, without compromising on its appearance.

Conclusion

The original specimen design clearly set out an elegant, slender, three-tower cable-stayed bridge destined to become one of the most famous bridges in the world in a location already famous for significant bridges. This presented a series of technical challenges to the design and construction teams who were charged with turning the client's vision into reality. Many of the design and construction solutions were based on tried and tested methods, but such is the scale of the Queensferry Crossing that the technologies deployed had to be taken to hitherto untried levels.

The result is a bridge which all involved are immeasurably proud to have been a part of and which will stand forever as a benchmark in bridge design and construction in the first half of the 21st century.

CHAPTER 4

The Sub-Structure

FCBC started construction work on the Queensferry Crossing in April 2011. As in all projects of such a scale, a considerable amount of planning preceded formal commencement of construction works on-site. Establishing offices, recruiting the team and defining working areas consumed most of the early period. The following chapters provide a description of how the bridge was actually built. The works have been split into three headings, broadly reflecting the organisation of the construction teams on-site:

- Sub-structure (this Chapter): the marine and land foundations, the towers, the V-shaped piers supporting the northern and southern approach viaducts and the abutments which form the transition between the super-structure and the land at the ends of the road deck
- Super-structure (Chapter 5): principally the road deck, the stay cables from which the road deck is suspended, the viaducts and all associated finishing works
- Network connections (Chapter 6): the road works north and south of the Firth of Forth which connect the new bridge to the existing trunk and local road network.

What is a cable-stayed bridge?

The Queensferry Crossing is a cable-stayed bridge. Since the late 20th century, cable-stayed technology has largely taken the place of the more traditional suspension bridge system in the design and construction of major bridges around the world. The Forth Road Bridge, opened by Her Majesty The Queen on 4th September 1964, is an excellent example of a traditional suspension bridge. The elegant curves of the main cables, the arc of the road deck and the vertical lines of the suspension cables are familiar features of this type of bridge the world over.

So, how does a cable-stayed bridge differ from a suspension bridge? The critical elements which make a suspension bridge function properly are the main cables which stretch from the land on either side before rising up and over the main towers. To these cables, a series of vertical suspender cables (called "hangers") are attached. These take the weight of the road deck suspended above the water. The main cables are the principal structural

1
Marine Operation Base
Rosyth Dockyard
Crew & Material Boarding

2
Cable Stayed Bridge Deck Yard
Segment Storage & Preparation

3
General Installations Yard
Concrete Batching Plant
Main Workshop
Storage/Carpentry/Steel Reinforcement

4
Main Project Office
(FCBC & Transport Scotland)

5
North Approach Viaduct

6
South Approach Viaduct

7
Echline Satellite Office

8
Queensferry Junction

elements of the bridge and are secured in position by means of massive concrete and steel anchors buried deep into the bedrock on land either side of the estuary. Notably, there is no direct link between the main cables and the road deck itself.

A cable-stayed bridge differs from a traditional suspension bridge in that the principal structural elements – the stay cables – are directly linked to the road deck. Instead of giant, land-based anchors, the cables holding the road deck up are actually anchored into the deck itself at one end and into a tower at the other. The load is transmitted via the cables directly from the road deck to the towers and down through the towers to the seabed. The elimination of land anchors is a major benefit of the cable-stayed concept. Cable-stayed bridges are also much stiffer than suspension bridges, so that deformations of the deck under wind and traffic loads are much less pronounced.

The other main advantage is ease of maintenance. Individual steel strands inside the cables can easily be removed and replaced as they reach the end of their operational life without requiring the closure of the bridge or affecting the bridge's viability or traffic flow in any way. This is not possible with a suspension bridge. A cost-effective, co-ordinated forward programme of

Above: **Night-time shots of the bridges of the Forth have a special appeal. By March 2016, the three cantilevers are progressing well.**

Below: **Comparison of suspension bridge and cable-stayed bridge designs.**

Suspension bridge

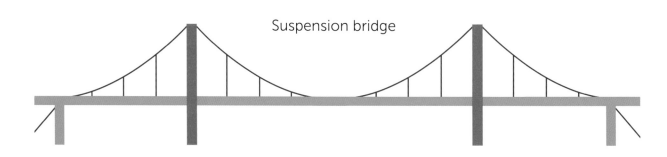

Red = compression   Blue = tension

Cable-stayed bridge

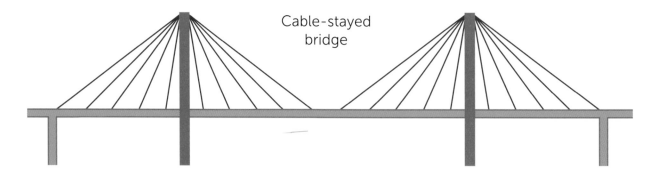

This page: **Three famous cable-stayed bridges, from top: Hong Kong's Stonecutters Bridge, the Rio Antirrio Bridge in Greece and the Millau Viaduct in France.**

maintenance can, therefore, be put in place and the reliable long term performance of the bridge guaranteed.

These days, cable-stayed bridges represent the cutting edge solution for many major new bridges worldwide, just as suspension bridges did for much of the previous two centuries. The Stonecutters Bridge in Hong Kong (2009), the Millau Viaduct in France (2004) and the Rio Antirrio bridge in Greece (2004) are all fine examples. The Queensferry Crossing goes one better. It has a unique feature which takes the technology of cable-stayed bridges to a new level: at the centre of each span, there is a length of deck, 140m long, where the cables descending from one tower cross with the cables coming from the neighbouring tower. This "crossover" represents a novel, 21st century solution to the need to provide stabilisation for the central tower in multi-span, cable-stayed bridges such as the Queensferry Crossing.

Foundations

Down the ages, one of the most important elements in the long term viability of any bridge structure has always been the foundations. In a cable-stayed bridge, such as the Queensferry Crossing, the quality of the foundations is critical to the stability of the towers which house the anchors for the cables from which the road deck is suspended. The approach viaducts, too, carrying traffic to and from the main bridge, require solid foundations to support similar heavy loads. Critical to the success of the

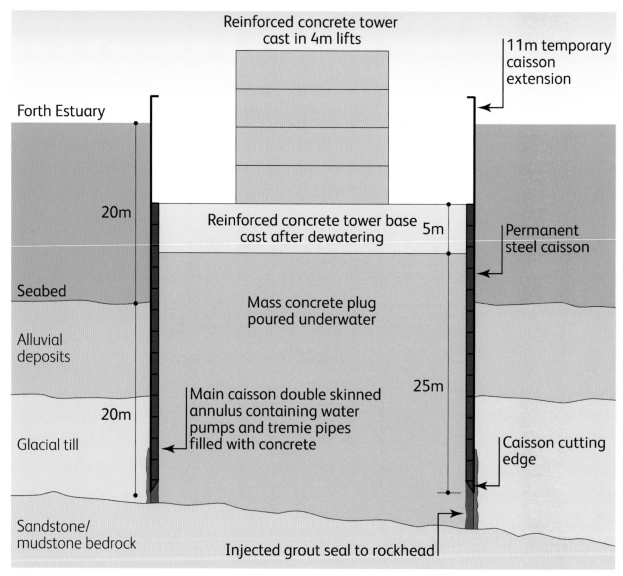

Reinforced concrete tower
cast in 4m lifts

11m temporary
caisson
extension

Forth Estuary

20m

Reinforced concrete tower base
cast after dewatering 5m

Permanent
steel caisson

Seabed

Alluvial
deposits

Mass concrete plug
poured underwater

Main caisson double skinned
annulus containing water
pumps and tremie pipes
filled with concrete

25m

20m

Glacial till

Caisson cutting
edge

Sandstone/
mudstone bedrock

Injected grout seal to rockhead

Above: Diagram showing the structure and positioning of the permanent foundation caissons, the temporary caissons, the tower bases and the positioning of the towers.

construction of the Queensferry Crossing's foundations were steel caissons and cofferdams to keep the sea out and allow works to be carried out 'in the dry'.

Caissons

Derived from the French word "caisse" meaning "box", a caisson is essentially a hollow, steel tube open at both ends. This is lowered into position into the seabed where it acts as a "mould" into which concrete can be poured creating the foundations. This concrete forms a direct link between the bedrock and the tower bases. Caissons do not represent new technology – after all, they were successfully deployed in the construction of both the Forth Bridge in the 1880s and the Forth Road Bridge in the 1950s

and 60s – but they do offer certain advantages over other techniques, such as piling, which could have been employed and were considered by FCBC. Working in deep water in an exposed location such as the Forth Estuary, the cylindrical caissons can be lowered from the surface to their final position on the seabed. Piling in such conditions would be a more difficult, more risky and time-consuming operation. Today, lowering caissons can be done relatively simply from cranes mounted on surface barges, a far cry from the 19th century system of sending down teams of deep-sea divers and human excavators working in a compressed air environment in appallingly cramped and dangerous conditions, sometimes at the cost of their lives.

On completion of their primary role, caissons remain in place as part of the foundations structure.

On the Queensferry Crossing, three enormous caissons were used: for the foundations of the North Tower, the

Left: A view of the Approach Viaduct South's V-shaped, reinforced concrete support piers.

Above: Early aerial view of cofferdam installation for the Approach Viaduct South's piers.

Below: The sheer scale of the three caissons is obvious in this photo taken in the fabrication yard in March 2012.

South Tower and Pier S1, the largest of the piers supporting the southern approach viaduct ("S" standing for "south").

Cofferdams

Cofferdams perform essentially the same function as caissons but are normally removed once the foundations

Above: **Looking up at the interior of one of the steel caisson panels during fabrication.**

Below: **May 2012, the arrival of the first two caissons in Rosyth Dock.**

Right: **Trial fitting of a temporary caisson on top of a permanent caisson in April 2012.**

have been completed. Cofferdams are better suited to foundations on land or in shallow water. However, unlike the cylindrical caissons which are pre-fabricated off-site before being delivered and installed, rectangular or circular cofferdams can be constructed on-site from sheet steel panels, corrugated for extra rigidity and with interlocking joints. Various construction methodologies were used for the Queensferry Crossing's cofferdams, those for the Central Tower and Pier S6 being built in situ while a further five (for Piers S2 to S5 and N1) were pre-fabricated off-site and floated into position by barge.

Other foundations

Finally, for those piers located on dry land, a third method of foundation construction was used – open excavation. Large excavations were dug into the ground, then backfilled with mass concrete to the required foundation profile. This created a secure "plug", similar in function to the plugs inside the caissons and cofferdams, on top of which a reinforced concrete base could be constructed. This, in turn, supports the pier structures built above, in 4.6m high sections, using climbing formwork as

Left: A historic moment as the first two caissons arrive on the Forth, May 2012.

Above: Peering down inside the North Tower caisson during fit out at Rosyth Docks, mid 2012.

Below: By summer 2012, the caissons were ready to be taken out to site and installation on the seabed could begin.

described below. Open excavations were used for the foundations of Pier N2 on the north side, Piers S7 and S8 on the south side as well as for both north and south abutments.

Fabrication and installation caissons

The Queensferry Crossing's three double-skinned caissons were fabricated by Polish fabricators, Crist, based in Gdynia near Gdansk. Their sheer scale was remarkable. The largest, used for the South Tower foundations was 30m high by 32m in diameter – approximately the height of an eight storey building. Its total weight was a massive 1,200 tonnes making it one of the largest steel caissons ever used anywhere in the world. Somebody calculated that there was room inside for three quarters of a million footballs. Somebody else took the trouble to work out that the entire population of Fife would fit inside though, perhaps

carrying two caissons arrived in May 2012 after a journey of seven days.

On arrival, the caissons were off-loaded from the barges and took up temporary residence in FCBC's yard in Rosyth Docks where, over a matter of four weeks, final preparations were made to the structures, including the removal of the sea fastenings and the installation of water pumping systems and electrical and lighting circuits and other infrastructure items.

After final checks and inspections were carried out, the caissons were ready to be taken out, one at a time, to their final destination on the seabed.

If the arrival on-site of the caissons represented the first

Top: Specially designed floating sheerleg cranes held the caissons in position during the lowering operation.

Above: The North Tower temporary caisson is fitted on top of the permanent caisson in September 2012.

Right: Mechanical grabs excavated over 90,000 cubic metres of seabed alluvium from each of the caissons.

major milestone for the Project, then the successful outcome of the installation and positioning process would be the second. Positioning such large structures accurately underwater was a critically important operation and a massive civil engineering task. The construction team would only have one chance to do it successfully.

Caisson installation

With final land-side preparations complete, each caisson was loaded on to a semi-submersible barge and transported downstream to a temporary location close to its final position where, having been slid off the barge and anchored, concrete was poured into the annulus, a one metre wide void between the inner and outer skins of the caisson, to provide strengthening of the cutting shoe (where the two skins meet at a sharp point down at the base of the caisson). Next, the caisson was guided into position by one of the world's largest floating sheerleg cranes specially designed for the purpose. This operation was made possible only because of the buoyancy afforded by the air-filled annulus which reduced the effective weight of the caisson in the water to around 500 tonnes against its actual weight of 1,200 tonnes. (see diagram on page 54)

Positioning each caisson to within a horizontal accuracy

mercifully, the precise methodology of this calculation was never revealed. Nor was the hypothesis ever put to the test.

Once the giant curved section plates of each caisson had been welded and bolted together to form the structure, a trial fitting of an 11m high, single-skinned caisson top extension was carried out, testing for a perfect, watertight seal. In situ later in the Firth of Forth, this temporary extension would prevent sea water from filling the interior of the caissons once they had been lowered and sunk into the seabed. Such advance trial fittings in the fabrication yard would ensure that the construction team would not encounter any problems on-site when fitting the temporary caissons for real out on the Forth.

Upon completion, the caissons were carefully moved on to specially designed, semi-submersible barges and transported to the Firth of Forth, where the first shipment

Above: One of the barges bringing fresh foundation concrete from the dockside batching plant to the caissons.

Right: Barge-mounted mixers kept the concrete at the right consistency for pumping into the caissons.

of 200mm was achieved through the use of the latest Global Positioning System (GPS) satellite technology as the caisson was slowly lowered approximately 20m down to meet the seabed. Water was then pumped into the annulus to act as ballast to increase the weight of the caisson and help sink the entire structure into the sedimentary alluvium lying on top of the bedrock. As depths increased and stiffer materials, such as boulder clay, were encountered, so extra weight became necessary to maintain the downward trajectory. On the largest caisson (at the South Tower), a total of 3,300 cubic metres of concrete was poured into the caisson's annulus, displacing the water that had previously been pumped in and greatly adding to the overall weight. This allowed the caisson to continue its journey down through the dense layers of clay and glacial till lying deep in the seabed. As it descended, the caisson would tilt first in one direction then, after correction by adding more concrete, in the other, the maximum tilt allowed being 3.5 degrees.

At this point, the construction team was made aware of the close interest being taken in the Project by members of the public, many of whom were moved to telephone the Project Hotline to point out that the caissons were going down "squint".

QUEENSFERRY PEOPLE

Jenny Symons

This article first appeared in the Queensferry Crossing's Project Update Newsletter of August 2012. Between 2011 and 2015, Jenny Symons was an Engineering Geologist with the Forth Crossing Design Joint Venture, FCBC's design partners.

Q What is your role on the Forth Replacement Crossing Project?

A I am essentially a "rock inspector". My job is to analyse the rock uncovered by the construction activity both on the seabed and on shore and compare the results against the many ground investigations carried out prior to construction works starting. This is important since, clearly, the new bridge is being built on rock and we need an accurate, detailed picture of the shape and strength of the rock formations which will support the foundations for the bridge's towers and piers – indeed, the entire weight of the bridge.

Q So, what types of rock is the new bridge being built on?

A The bedrock beneath the waters of the Forth is made up of a series of multi-layered – or 'interbedded' – sedimentary rock strata (layers) including sandstone, limestone, mudstone and siltstone. These rocks were formed during a geological time period known as the Carboniferous Period and are up to 360 million years old. The layers of sedimentary rock are interrupted in many places by another type of rock called dolerite. This is an igneous rock which is associated with volcanic activity that occurred in this part of Scotland millions of years ago. The molten

dolerite was originally forced upwards from the bowels of the earth and squeezed in between the layers of sedimentary rock. You can see the dolerite rock exposed in the walls of the cutting on the Fife side of the existing A90.

Beamer Rock in the middle of the Forth is made of dolerite. The geological structure of the area is marked by a series of faults associated with tectonic plate movements which have caused the rock strata to be offset and tilted away from horizontal. The bedrock is topped by a layer, over 20 metres thick in places, of superficial material including alluvium (soft, sandy clay or silt containing gravel and shells, deposited by historic flood events), glacial till (stiff clay with sand, gravel and occasional cobbles and boulders, deposited by melting glacial ice), and fluvioglacial material (sands and gravels in glacial till that has been moved and re-deposited by rivers). Together, this material is called sediment.

Q What are the main challenges on a job like this?

A Working out at sea – and beneath the water – is never easy. The excavation process, which creates a space on the sea bed for the tower and pier foundations, is carried out underwater and so the machine operators are essentially working "blind", relying on what their instruments tell them (about the depth to rock etc.) rather than what they can see. The divers carrying out inspections on the seabed are restricted by tidal and weather conditions. They carry CCTV cameras which send pictures up to the surface for people like me to view. Before we can pour concrete to start constructing the foundations, the rock surface must be clean – ie. free of sediment, loose rocks and other material.

Q What gives you most satisfaction?

A That's easy – every day on this job we are having it confirmed that the ground model or "geological map" we drew up on the basis of our detailed ground investigations is, in fact, extremely accurate. The design of the bridge was greatly influenced by these geological investigations and encountering no surprises means that the construction of the bridge can proceed with a minimum of re-design being necessary, if any at all. This, in turn, minimises any delays in the construction programme. It is good to know that we got it right and that all the effort and time spent on the ground investigations was well worth it.

Above: Lorries loading up with fresh concrete at the on-site batching plant in Rosyth, one of the most modern in Europe.

Left: From the barges, liquid concrete was pumped through pipes and poured over steel reinforcement bars known as 'rebar'.

the Firth of Forth where it was returned to the seabed under licence. The internal excavation reduced the friction between the caisson walls and the seabed, thus helping to lower the structure. As they descended, the caissons were minutely monitored to ensure they were going down vertically, any tilt being constantly corrected by careful ballasting and further excavation.

A vertical rib feature on the outside of the caissons ensured that a gap was created further reducing friction between the structure and the adjacent seabed. Bentonite (a compound of clay and water) was injected down into this gap to create and maintain a slippery, friction-reduced interface. Meanwhile, high-pressure water jets loosened the ground ahead of the cutting edge at the base of the caisson further easing its course downwards. Constant GPS monitoring resulted in all three caissons successfully reaching their final resting place within the allowable tolerances. And not squint!

Encountering unforeseen boulders in the alluvial and

The lowering operations were aided by excavations taking place inside the caissons. Using floating cranes with mechanical grabs, each capable of lifting ten tonnes of material in every scoop, a total of 92,000 cubic metres of excavated seabed was removed from inside all three caissons. This material was removed by barge to one of two designated areas of deep water further downstream in

After de-watering, a view inside the North Tower caisson to the top of the 25 metre deep concrete foundation 'plug'.

The reinforced concrete base of the North Tower was created on top of the 'plug'. Here, rebar reinforcement has been positioned ready for pouring the first Tower section.

Above: **Preparations complete for the pouring of the first section of the Central Tower in September 2013.**

Left: **Inside the Central Tower foundation cofferdam.**

Below: **One of the team of divers prepares to inspect the bedrock during caisson installation.**

glacial deposits was the main risk associated with the successful completion of the sinking operations. Careful advance ultrasound analysis and ground inspections carried out by divers using sonar equipment greatly mitigated this risk by producing accurate maps of the geology of the river bed beneath the waters of the Forth.

The caissons were sunk to a level 1m to 3m above the sloping bedrock where they were held stable by the friction and firmness of the stiffer soils at that depth. Next, a 3m to 5m high seal was formed right around the bottom of the caisson walls by pumping a ring of 120 jet-grouted columns, 1.5m in diameter, down through 200mm drill tubes attached to each caisson's outer wall. This jet grouting created a strong seal between the caisson and the sloping bedrock, thus preventing sea water and sediment seeping back in. Once the seal had been secured, the remaining material lying over the bedrock inside the caisson was removed using a powerful airlift acting like an underwater vacuum cleaner. The interior excavations continued underwater until all the seabed alluvium had been removed and the bedrock itself was exposed to view through remotely controlled underwater cameras and ready for inspection by divers. During the sinking process, the 11m high temporary caissons were fitted on top of each caisson, keeping the top rim of the combined structures well above sea-level at all times thereby allowing later construction activities to be carried out in the dry.

By the summer of 2013, the excavations had been completed and the rock surfaces inside the caissons cleared of all loose debris. A completely clean rock surface was vital to enable a thorough inspection of the bedrock to be undertaken and to allow a good bond to be achieved between the rock and the concrete which was about to be placed inside the caisson to start forming the foundations. The next stage was to pour thousands of cubic metres of specially prepared concrete suitable for underwater use into each caisson up to various heights (a maximum of 26m in the case of the South Tower) to form a solid, watertight "plug". Amongst its other characteristics, this concrete does not mix with or contaminate the water. Staying in place forever, the caissons become a permanent element of the foundations acting as a shield protecting the concrete bases not only from the ravages of the sea but also ship impact.

It is worth noting that almost all of the concrete used in the construction of the Queensferry Crossing, including that used in the foundations, the towers, the viaduct piers and the reinforced deck, was produced in FCBC's specially designed and constructed, fully computerised and automated batching plant in Rosyth Docks, one of the most modern such facilities in Europe. In all, across almost five years in operation, the plant produced in excess of 200,000 cubic metres of concrete (around half a million tonnes)

with an impressive 99.8% quality compliance – a proud record. Transporting the concrete from the dockside batching plant to where it was needed out in mid estuary while maintaining the correct flow characteristics so that, once there, it could be successfully pumped – and often twice or even thrice pumped - presented considerable logistical difficulties. The challenge was overcome through the use of a fleet of four, specially commissioned barges, each holding six 12 cubic metre capacity static concrete mixers on board into which the freshly batched concrete was pumped from a fleet of wagons bringing the fresh concrete from the batching plant (see photos on page 62).

During every concrete pour, it was vital that the concrete be delivered to site in a timely manner that allowed the several thousand cubic metres to be poured in a constant flow, enabling it to set in one homogenous block and to ensure it settled correctly with no air pockets within the concrete mass, thus achieving its required strength. This was successfully achieved by having the four barges in constant, 24 hour use in a sea-borne cycle for several days on end: the first barge loading up with concrete at the quayside, the second making its way out to site, the third at site discharging its load of concrete, and the fourth making its way back to dock in order to pick up a fresh load. On arrival at the tower sites, the concrete was first pumped into tanks situated on the barge moored alongside the caisson from where it was pumped down into the bottom of the water-filled caisson via "tremie" pipes. These pipes are designed to be easily moved around inside the structure to ensure an even coverage and were withdrawn upwards in stages as the concrete rose displacing the clean water inside the caisson which was pumped out over the top of the caisson and back into the sea.

A notable world record was achieved in September 2013. The operation to create the concrete plug inside the South Tower caisson required a total of 16, 869 cubic metres of concrete to be poured in a non-stop, continuous operation which lasted 15 days and nights. This represented the world's largest ever continuous underwater concrete pour and, it is believed, the third largest concrete pour of any kind ever undertaken. The weight of the concrete poured was almost 40,000 tonnes, the equivalent of 3,250 London double-decker buses (without passengers). The barges delivering the concrete for this operation notched up 273 separate journeys between the dock and the caisson, covering approximately 1,800km (further than the distance between John o' Groats and Land's End).

Across all three caissons, the total weight of concrete poured was over 90,000 tonnes.

Once the underwater concrete plugs had been poured inside each caisson, a significant milestone for the Project as a whole, the remaining sea water not already displaced

Above: **The South Tower foundation team celebrates the largest ever continuous underwater concrete pour.**

by the rising concrete was pumped out of the caissons allowing the interior and the top of the concrete plugs to dry. The top three inches of concrete were then removed to create a good quality surface "key" on which to start the next stage of construction, the 14m deep reinforced concrete bases for the towers.

Central tower cofferdam

The Central Tower of the Queensferry Crossing, unlike its neighbours, the North and South Towers, has its foundations not in a caisson but in a 30m long, 10-piece, octagonal cofferdam anchored deep in the Beamer Rock, a dolerite rock outcrop in the middle of the Forth which is exposed during low tide. To a large extent, the very existence of this small, conveniently located rock island, the site of a miniature navigational lighthouse, was responsible for the final positioning of the bridge: in a multi-span bridge such as the Queensferry Crossing having the middle tower founded on solid rock brings significant advantages in terms of stability. Interestingly, a similar outcrop had determined the position of the Forth Bridge 130 years previously.

In order to create a watertight cofferdam into which the Central Tower's reinforced concrete foundations could be laid, it was first necessary to remove the Beamer Rock navigational light (later to be rebuilt at an alternative location on shore) before blasting a hole 6m deep in which

the cofferdam could be constructed. A total of 5,000 cubic metres of rock was removed. Powerful rotary cutters levelled and then cut a chase into the rock floor. Each pre-formed, 10.7m high, L-shaped panel with reinforced concrete base and steel sheet pile wall was loaded on to a barge and transported to site. The panels were lifted into position, aided by tie down anchors in the rock which slotted into holes in the concrete base, and were jacked to a pre-determined level just above the blasted rock formation. Once the units were laid down onto the supporting shims to the desired level and fixed into position, underwater concrete was placed to fill the gap between the precast unit and the rock. The gaps in the sheet pile cofferdam were then infilled with individual sheet piles and the joints sealed. The cofferdam was then de-watered and 4,000 cubic metres of reinforced concrete was poured in to form the foundation of the Central Tower. Being securely situated on the bedrock of the Beamer Rock, an underwater concrete plug, such as was created beneath the North and South Tower foundations, was not required.

Throughout the entire Queensferry Crossing Project, the concrete batching team received invaluable help from colleagues in FCBC's fully accredited Testing Laboratory where every batch of concrete was subject to a variety of

Cofferdam

Central Tower

Beamer Rock

Top left: Diagram showing the positioning of the Central Tower foundation cofferdam on Beamer Rock.

Top right: The Central Tower cofferdam almost complete.

Above: One of the 10.7 metre high, steel sheet pile panels which made up the Central Tower cofferdam.

tests designed to guarantee its suitability for the specific task it was designed for. Together, the batching plant and laboratory staff enabled the construction teams out on-site to do their job to world class standards.

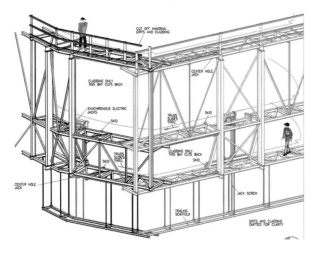

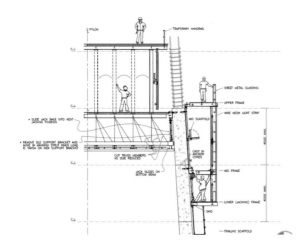

Above: Diagrams showing the structure of the temporary 'jump forms' used to form the concrete moulds for each tower.

Right: Mid 2014, the jump form sits on top of the South Tower just above road deck level. Beneath, temporary steel trestles are installed to support the initial road deck sections.

Towers

The concrete plugs inside the North and South Tower caissons and the Central Tower cofferdam created the immensely heavy, strong and secure platforms needed to support the foundations of the three towers for the lifespan of the bridge. By the autumn of 2013, the mass concrete foundation work inside the caissons and Central Tower cofferdam was complete and the marine foundations essentially finished. This meant the focus of construction work was no longer downwards towards the seabed, but could turn upwards to face the sky. Work could now get underway on the construction of the bridge's three towers.

The scale of the task facing the team was daunting. The three towers were destined to become the tallest bridge towers anywhere in the UK. Indeed, the tallest of them, the Central Tower, at a fraction over 210m Above Ordnance

Datum (AOD) is up to 60m – or 38% - higher than the towers of the neighbouring Forth Road Bridge and almost exactly double the height of the Forth Bridge's famous steel cantilevers. The North and South Towers each top out at 202m AOD.

Other statistics are equally impressive. The Central Tower comprises 8,900 cubic metres of reinforced concrete, slightly less - 8,500 cubic metres - for the two flanking towers. The Central Tower contains a total of 2,500 tonnes of steel reinforcement inside the concrete base and tower walls (1,800 tonnes for each of the other towers). All three towers also house 400 tonnes of steel anchor boxes which provide the anchor points for fixing the bridge's all-important stay cables to the towers. These are significant weights to be borne by such slender structures. In addition, the hollow towers taper gracefully as

Weather on the bridge

As with all aspects of the construction of the Queensferry Crossing, a major challenge faced by the construction teams was weather, in particular wind since so much activity involved lifting and working at height. Regular, accurate weather forecasts were vital to the effective planning and efficient execution of the works.

From day one, FCBC worked closely with the Met Office whose detailed forecasts, particularly concerning wind, enabled advanced work schedules to be drawn up, thus reducing as far as possible the negative impact of poor weather conditions on the schedule.

This case study article was supplied by the Met Office and first appeared in the Project Update newsletter of February 2014.

"This is a fantastic project which will produce one of the biggest road bridges in the United Kingdom. Almost everything we do out on the waters of the Forth is weather dependent, so it is vitally important – not least to the health and safety of our construction personnel – that we have dependable, accurate and site-specific forecasts with which to plan our work schedules"

Ken Clark, FCBC Marine Liaison Officer

Met Office case study

We are providing critical weather and climate forecast services to FCBC, the construction consortium building the new cable-stayed road bridge across the Firth of Forth in Scotland. Our detailed information helps deliver efficiencies within the build project and manage health and safety on-site by ensuring the construction consortium is aware of any weather-related risks.

The prevailing wind in this area is from the west (the Atlantic influence) but as the Forth flows into the North Sea there are times when this relatively cold body of water has a considerable effect on the local weather throughout the year. From April to September, poor visibility, caused by a fog from the North Sea known locally as 'haar', can occur around the bridge despite the weather being fine and sunny just a short distance away. In addition, although the east coast of Scotland has a fairly low rainfall (640mm as an annual average)

July and August can be very wet locally. The new bridge and the surrounding area are susceptible to strong winds and icy conditions, especially during winter.

The FCBC team was aware of the challenges that weather brings to the existing bridge and approached us to help mitigate the impacts of the weather on the construction plan and build.

Solution

In the pre-construction phase, we conducted a study of the proposed replacement bridge site, using the Met Office's Virtual Met Mast™ (VMM), a site-specific wind prediction solution, together with a general climate assessment from the nearby Edinburgh Gogarbank meteorological observing site.

We ran a VMM analysis at two locations on the north and south sides of the bridge, for heights of 10m, 50m, 100m and 200m above ground level. The VMM analysis report gave detailed information on the climate of the build site, identified times of day when winds would potentially be at their highest and lowest speeds; times of year when wind shear would be at its greatest and least; as well as providing a rainfall analysis of the build site. This information enabled the construction team to evaluate and refine its structural designs to best mitigate any impact of the weather, and the project management team to assess schedules for the construction phase.

For the build phase, FCBC is utilising a combination of forecasts and planning tools from the Met Office. The project management team receives a five-day site-specific forecast giving a detailed weather synopsis on an hourly breakdown for the first day, supported by a three-hourly breakdown for days two and three, and finally a six-hourly breakdown for days four and five.

The team uses WeatherWindows, the Met Office's web-based planning tool, to plan weather-dependent tasks up to 15 days ahead. WeatherWindows automatically monitors and displays the best time periods when tasks can be carried out, aiding resource planning by showing the best opportunities to carry out particular tasks. Only information directly relevant to FCBC's planning needs is displayed.

In addition, Met Office forecasts for elevations of 50m, 100m and 200m provide wind speed, direction and maximum gust information. These forecasts help the FCBC team to plan and monitor activities when people are working at height and ensure compliance with health and safety regulations.

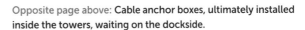

Opposite page above: Cable anchor boxes, ultimately installed inside the towers, waiting on the dockside.

Opposite page below: Blasting on Beamer Rock to excavate a hole in which the foundation cofferdam would be constructed.

Above left: One of the anchor boxes being lifted into position on the North Tower.

Left: View of the South Tower jump form. Note tower shaft disappearing into the mist.

Above: A new section of a tower crane mast is lifted into position during erection.

they rise from a footprint of 16m by 14m at the base to 7.5m by 5.0m at the top. The thickness of the tower walls decreases from 1.6m at the base to 0.90m at the top. The total weight of the Central Tower is 22,000 tonnes. Taken together, the Queensferry Crossing's three towers contain over 25,000 cubic metres of reinforced concrete and over 6,000 tonnes of steel reinforcement.

So, how do you build these giants? The first task – as, indeed, two years later the very last task at the top of the completed towers – involved a concrete pour. As we have seen, each tower sits on a reinforced concrete base which is placed directly on top of the previously created concrete plug deep inside the – now de-watered - caissons (or cofferdam for the Central Tower). This 9m deep reinforced base is constructed using an intricate mesh of steel reinforcement bars (known as "rebar") into which approximately 4,000 cubic metres of concrete is poured to create an immensely strong structure in which the first vertical section of the tower can be accommodated.

Work began first on the Central Tower in July 2013, followed in the autumn by the North Tower and finally, at the end of the year, by the South Tower.

The towers were built in 4m high sections, called "lifts",

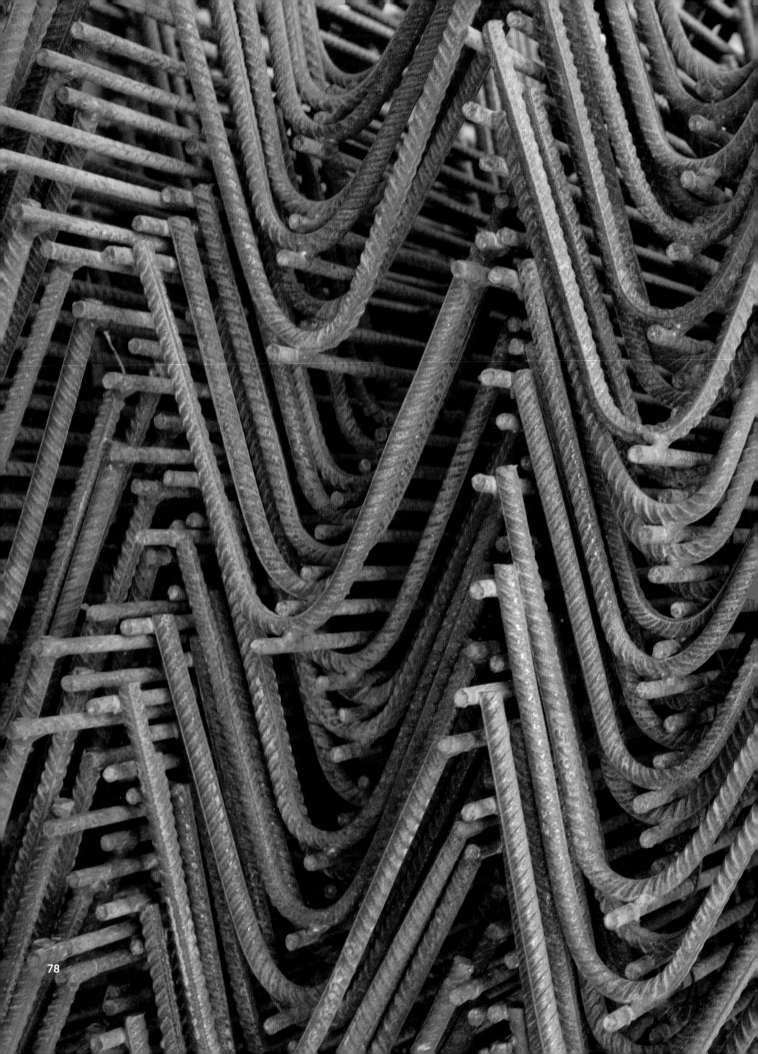

Queensferry Crossing   Edinburgh   2015

Bridging the Forth
Safely

202m + 210m + 202m
Highest Bridge Towers in the UK

Opposite and this page: Cause for celebration: autumn 2015 saw the topping out of all three towers – far left, South Tower; above, North Tower; below, Central Tower.

each completed lift creating a hollow ring of reinforced concrete capable of bearing the weight of the next lift above. In total, each tower had 54 lifts.

Concrete was poured into a temporary structure - essentially a mould - filled with rebar reinforcement "cages" pre-assembled at FCBC's dockside yard. Made from steel and timber, this temporary structure is known as a "jump form". "Jump" because, at the end of each lift, it can jump higher, by means of hydraulic jacks, in readiness for the next lift, and "form" because it forms the correct concrete shape within its internal and external faces.

The jump form system on the Queensferry Crossing was overseen by FCBC's Temporary Works Department working with a specialist subcontractor and was designed to be easily adaptable in size. As each tapering tower rises section by section, so the steelfixers and joiners could make incremental adjustments to the reinforcement cages and

The Sub-Structure

Above: **Early 2016, the view from the crew boat returning to land after another shift out on the towers.**

jump form to achieve the desired profile. Once the concrete in each lift had gained sufficient strength to support itself, typically 36 hours, the adjusted shutters could be jacked up hydraulically in preparation for the next concrete pour. Typically, the cycle time for each 4m lift, taking into account the moving and setting up of the climbing formwork, the rebar installation, the concrete pour and the concrete setting, was about 12 days. Depending on weather conditions, at times a weekly cycle was achieved.

As the towers rose, it was necessary to incorporate the steel cable anchor boxes, the first of these being installed with the 38th lift at a height of 152m. These boxes, lifted up into position by the tower cranes, were fitted with starter pipes which formed holes in the walls through which the stay cables would be later threaded and anchored.

Around the outside of the jump form, a secure 11m tall steel and wooden framework was fixed which, in addition to providing secure conditions for the construction team to work safely at height and offering protection against the

vagaries of the weather, also housed all the necessary infrastructure, such as power supply, lighting systems and concrete pumps, to facilitate work on each lift. Taken together with the jump form inside, the entire tower top structures were known as "birdcages" and became one of the most prominent features of the emerging new bridge as the towers rose ever higher. Electrically powered jacks raised the birdcages up 4m with each lift, while the configuration of the plywood-faced, steel-framed shutters of the formwork was adjusted to take into account the tower's tapering profile.

Construction teams accessed the birdcages by means of two 12-man "Alimak" hoists, orange in colour, which ran on vertical tracks attached to the side of each tower, one below road deck level, one above. In addition, the permanent internal steel stairway was fabricated and erected inside the towers as they rose providing alternative access up and down. Permanent internal lifts were installed inside the towers only towards the end of the Project.

Throughout the tower construction phase, the seemingly endless demand for concrete from the construction teams on each tower was met by freshly batched concrete from the batching plant delivered on a

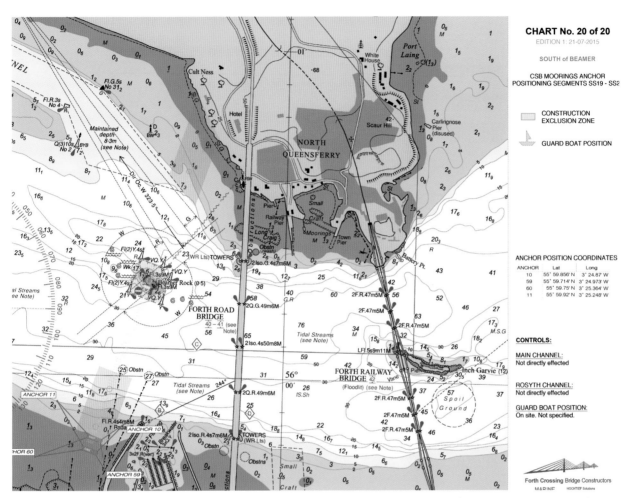

CHART No. 20 of 20
EDITION 1: 21-07-2015

SOUTH of BEAMER

CSB MOORINGS ANCHOR
POSITIONING SEGMENTS SS19 - SS2

CONSTRUCTION
EXCLUSION ZONE

GUARD BOAT POSITION

ANCHOR POSITION COORDINATES

ANCHOR	Lat	Long
10	55° 59.856' N	3° 24.87' W
59	55° 59.714' N	3° 24.973' W
60	55° 59.75' N	3° 25.364' W
11	55° 59.92' N	3° 25.248' W

CONTROLS:

MAIN CHANNEL:
Not directly effected

ROSYTH CHANNEL:
Not directly effected

GUARD BOAT POSITION:
On site. Not specified.

Forth Crossing Bridge Constructors
MARINE   HOCHTIEF Solutions

Above: A plan of the Forth estuary showing sea lanes and preferred routes for Queensferry Crossing marine plant.

reduced fleet of barges now catering for smaller quantities than the gluttonous foundations. Initially, the concrete was pumped directly into the tower shutters, until the first four deck sections were in place at each tower. Then, a secondary pump was attached to vertical pipework in the tower and the concrete was pumped – at 3,000lbs/sq inch pressure – to a 360 degree distributor fixed to the tower shutter. As the towers neared their final height over 200m above the waters of the Forth, the weight of liquid concrete inside the pipes at any one time was a massive six tonnes, so the pumping of the concrete was an extremely challenging operation in its own right.

Tower cranes

It was often assumed by external observers that the concrete for each new section of tower was lifted up by the tall, yellow cranes rising parallel to the towers. In fact, these tower cranes performed a range of other functions including lifting rebar cages, concreting equipment, temporary works materials, new sections of internal stairway, cable anchor boxes and cable tensioning equipment. They were never employed in the pouring of tower concrete other than the

very last, small parapet pours to complete the tower tops.

The tower cranes, weighing 450 tonnes and with a maximum lift capacity of 40 tonnes had separate foundations driven into the seabed. At regular vertical intervals, the cranes were firmly attached to the adjacent tower using a series of steel "ties". Each crane rose section by section, keeping above the height of the towers, each new section being lifted into place by the crane itself before being secured into position using high tensile steel bolts. The process was reversed in the spring of 2017 when the cranes had fulfilled their role and had to be removed. In common with all parts of the construction works, the tower cranes were subject to detailed daily and weekly inspections, as well as regular servicing, to ensure strict compliance with site safety and the manufacturer's operating standards.

The three tower cranes rose to become the highest cranes anywhere in the UK with a final maximum height of 235m and, since they projected themselves into the Edinburgh Airport airspace envelope, separate civil aviation

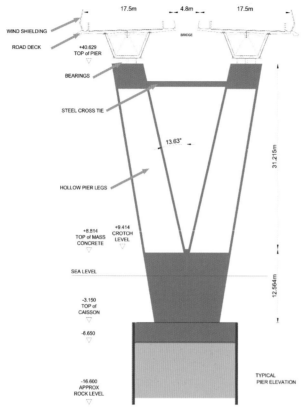

WIND SHIELDING

ROAD DECK

17.5m   4.8m   17.5m

BRIDGE

+40.629
TOP of PIER

BEARINGS

STEEL CROSS TIE

13.63°

HOLLOW PIER LEGS

+8.814   +9.414
TOP of MASS   CROTCH
CONCRETE   LEVEL

SEA LEVEL

-3.150
TOP of
CAISSON

-6.650

-16.600
APPROX
ROCK LEVEL

31.215m

12.564m

TYPICAL
PIER ELEVATION

Above: Diagram showing the structure of the V-shaped, reinforced concrete piers supporting the approach viaducts.

approvals and conditions were required.

Tower Topping Out

Throughout 2015, excitement mounted as the towers rose higher and higher towards their ultimate height. It was tempting for local residents to see the vertical progress being made out in the middle of the estuary as a race between the three tower construction teams. In truth, it was no race, the various stages of the works being carefully scheduled in advance across all three towers according to the needs of each. In the event, all three towers were completed on schedule within just a few weeks of each other. The first to successfully "top out", in October 2015, was the North Tower. The following month it was the turn of the South Tower before the Central Tower was completed in December (see photos on pages 80 and 81), marking perhaps the most significant milestone to date in the construction of the Queensferry Crossing and sparking much celebration.

Viaduct piers

Standing on either shore looking at the Queensferry Crossing, the most obvious features near to land are the V-shaped, reinforced concrete piers which support the north

and south approach viaducts. There are ten piers in total, two on the north and eight on the south shore. Just as with the cable-stayed bridge structure itself and the three towers, foundations built on bedrock were vital to the construction and stability of the viaduct piers.

Foundations

Three types of foundation were used. Firstly, for the largest of the piers on the south side - Pier S1 – which sits in deep water next to the South Tower and has the greatest depth down to bedrock, an enormous steel caisson similar to those used for the North and South Towers was used. In an installation process identical to that described above, the caisson was lowered to the seabed and back-filled with concrete poured underwater. Subsequently, the caisson was de-watered and a reinforced concrete base poured out of which the pier could grow.

For the piers situated in shallower water or on the tidal reaches of the estuary, cofferdams were used to form the foundations. These were constructed from corrugated steel sheet piles fabricated into a heavily braced rectangular structure and lowered down into concrete-filled trenches in a previously dredged area. The boxes were partially filled with mass concrete on top of which the reinforced concrete piers and their bases were built. In some of the shallower foundations, the sheet piles were individually driven to a predetermined depth to form the cofferdam.

Lastly, for Piers S8 and S7 and Pier N2 which are on dry land, open excavations exposed the bedrock upon which the concrete base and the pier could be constructed.

As the foundations for each pier were completed, so the construction of the pier itself could begin. A similar process was employed to the construction of the bridge's towers, the two legs of each pier being constructed in rising sections of reinforced concrete 4.6m in height. Temporary "climbing formwork" was used to shape the sections, the formwork being altered in size according to the changing geometry of the pier legs which tapered as they rose. Between the legs of the piers, steel cross-member ties were inserted near the top in order to increase the strength of the structure and reduce the amount of reinforcing steel required in the concrete.

Abutments

The final piece of the sub-structure jigsaw was the construction of the abutments. Abutments are large concrete structures built into the land at either end of the bridge on top of which the road deck rests.

Abutments have a number of functions. As well as providing vertical and lateral support for the bridge, they act as retaining walls to contain the in-fill which supports the approach roads. They carry bearings and movement joints which allow the bridge to expand and contract with

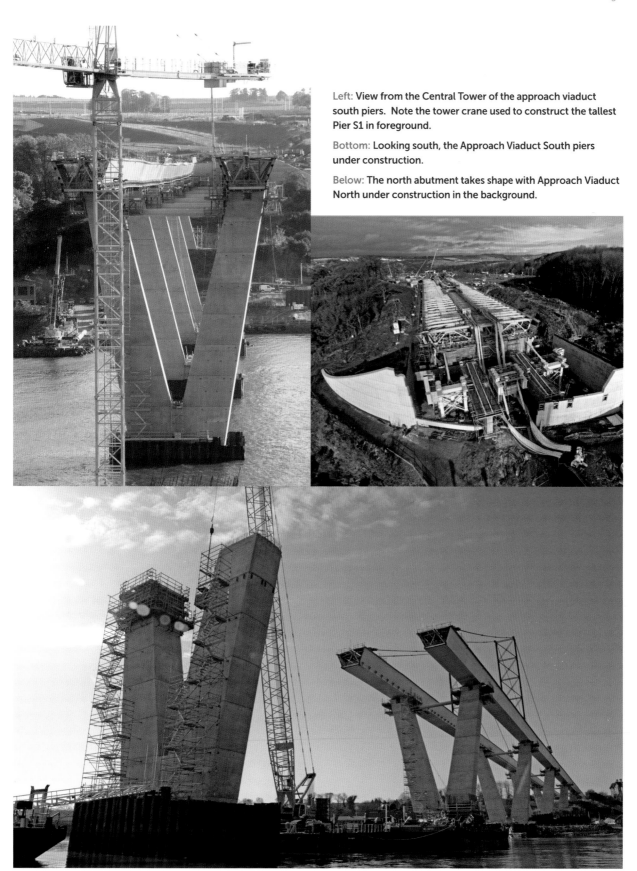

Left: View from the Central Tower of the approach viaduct south piers. Note the tower crane used to construct the tallest Pier S1 in foreground.

Bottom: Looking south, the Approach Viaduct South piers under construction.

Below: The north abutment takes shape with Approach Viaduct North under construction in the background.

temperature and wind and traffic load fluctuations. More prosaically, they also provide the bridge's maintenance team with internal access to the inside of the road deck. In addition, on the Queensferry Crossing, the south abutment contains offices, stores, garage space and equipment for maintenance purposes. The north abutment also contains offices and stores.

Marine

The Queensferry Crossing is located in the middle of one of the busiest shipping routes in the UK. Its southern main span sits astride the Forth Deepwater Channel, the main access to the ports upstream, principally Grangemouth which is Scotland's main oil port and home to one of the biggest petrochemical plants in Europe. It is also a busy container port, handling trade with North America and Europe. Meanwhile, the northern main span crosses the approach channel into the Port of Rosyth and the former Rosyth Naval Base. Built into the already complex brief for the construction of the new bridge was the requirement to keep these shipping lanes safe and open at all times.

FCBC's Marine Liaison Department was responsible for co-ordinating all marine movements throughout the construction phase of the Project. Through constant contact with the Forth & Tay Navigation Service, part of Forth Ports Authority and the River Forth's traffic controllers, all Queensferry Crossing ship and barge movements were timed so as to enable the team to safely carry out their operations unhindered while dovetailing, 24 hours a day, with all other major vessel movements, the activities of other river users and, in the summer months especially, the regular arrivals and departures of cruise liners carrying passengers keen to visit the historic sites, shops and restaurants of Edinburgh.

Between 2011 and Project completion in 2017, many thousands of seaborne vessel movements took place between FCBC's land and marine-based operations. Careful planning, constant vigilance, staff training, daily briefings and close communication with Forth Ports all contributed to a harmonious co-existence between the parties and no serious incidents occurred.

Below: **Pier N2, the first of the two Approach Viaduct North support piers, nears completion.**

CHAPTER 5
The Super-Structure

THE super-structure of a bridge is defined as those parts of the finished structure which enable the specific purpose for which the bridge has been built to be performed, in the case of the Queensferry Crossing the efficient and swift passage of vehicular traffic north and south across the Firth of Forth. In this chapter, we will look at the construction of the road deck, the installation of the stay cables (one of the signature features of the bridge) and the construction of the northern and southern approach viaducts.

Of course, the super-structure has another task to fulfil. In addition to carrying traffic and wind load (the "live" load), it also has to carry its own weight (the "dead" load). The Queensferry Crossing's suitability for this job stems from its stay cables: if one of the stay cables, or strands within it, has to be removed for maintenance or repair purposes, then the cables either side are capable of taking up the load and supporting the road deck with no necessary adverse effects on traffic flow. This is one of the principal advantages of a cable-stayed bridge.

Road deck

At 2.7km (1.6 miles), the road deck across the Queensferry Crossing is fractionally longer than that of the Forth Road Bridge next door, itself the longest suspension bridge outside the United States when it was opened in 1964. The Queensferry Crossing has entered the record books as the longest three-tower cable-stayed bridge in the world.

The road deck was constructed from 122 separate steel box-girder sections with an average weight of about 750 tonnes when lifted up into position up to 60m above the waters of the Forth. A standard section measures 16.2m long by 39.8m wide, meaning the deck area on each would easily accommodate a full-sized tennis court. Each section is 4.9m in depth.

The easiest way to understand how the road deck was constructed is to follow a typical deck section all the way from its fabrication and transportation to site and on to its

Above: Demonstrating its cross-section structure, a deck section is lifted up into position on the South Tower in May 2016.

Top right: Multiple deck sections take shape in the fabrication yard in China. Match fitting was important to ensure tight fit-up tolerances were achieved on-site.

Middle right: Celebrating the completion of the final – 122nd - deck section fabrication in June 2014.

Below: A shipment of deck sections and temporary formwork arrives at Rosyth.

final preparation and ultimate permanent installation on the bridge. Deck construction was carried out in three main stages: fabrication (off-site), final preparation (on-site) and installation.

Fabrication

All 122 deck sections were fabricated at the ZPMC steel fabrication plant near Shanghai in China, one of the most modern plants of its type anywhere in the world and one of the few capable of meeting an order of the magnitude demanded by the Queensferry Crossing. In recent times,

ZPMC have fabricated steel deck sections for many bridges throughout the world.

To ensure consistency of quality and help resolve any technical issues on the ground, fabrication was overseen by a team comprising personnel from FCBC, their designers, the EDT and an independent quality assurance company. Many members of staff were based permanently in China for the duration of the fabrication process.

Upon completion and before leaving the yard, every deck section was trial fitted to its neighbours to make sure that a perfect fit would be achievable on-site in the Firth of

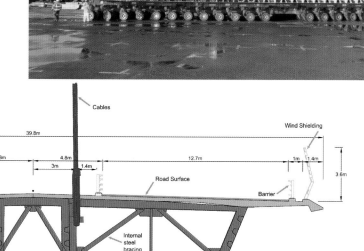

Above and right: Once unloaded from the ship, each deck section was moved into the dockside storage area by self-propelled modular transporters (SPMT).

Below: A diagram showing the structure of a deck section, including the top concrete surface and the position of the stay cables (blue).

Cables

Wind Shielding

39.8m

1.4m 1m   12.7m   4.8m   4.8m   12.7m   1m 1.4m

3m   1.4m   3.6m

Concrete deck

Road Surface

Barrier

Internal steel bracing

Structural steel tub

Above: Another deck segment is offloaded from the ship on to the dockside.

Left: Inside the fabrication yard where reinforced concrete was added to the deck sections on which the final road surface would eventually be laid.

the initial road deck sections to be installed (see below).

On arrival at Rosyth Docks, the deck sections were off-loaded on to the quayside and carefully manoeuvred into FCBC's 50,000 square metre storage yard, the equivalent of seven full-sized football pitches, by two remote-controlled SPMTs (self-propelled modular transporters) capable of transporting over 1,200 tonnes. Each section was positioned on temporary concrete plinths roughly 1.5m in height, allowing the low-slung SPMTs access underneath.

Final Preparation On-site

At this point, each deck section weighed an average of 250 tonnes (the maximum was 320 tonnes) and was essentially a structural steel box closed at the base and the sides but open at the ends and the top. The next stage was the casting of a reinforced concrete deck across the open top of the section. It is this deck which would ultimately carry the new bridge's final road surface. At the same time, the concrete wings which carry the hard shoulders were cast, cantilevered out five metres beyond the edge of the steel sections.

Forth. Happily, thanks to the accuracy of the design specifications, the expertise of the ZPMC staff and the Project team's focus on quality and getting everything right first time, any issues with fit were very rare and quickly sorted at ZPMC's yard, making the task of final installation in Scotland that much easier.

In April 2014, the first of seven shipments of deck sections left China bound for Rosyth, an approximately 12,000 nautical mile voyage that would take 47 days. Also on board the first shipment were the temporary steel "trestles" and platforms which would be attached to both sides of the bridge's growing towers to provide support for

Josh Ishibashi

Why steel?

Steel has been used in bridge construction for over 150 years. In an article which first appeared in the Queensferry Crossing's Project Update newsletter in February 2014, Joshua Ishibashi, FCBC Senior Cable-Stayed Bridge Super-Structure Engineer, explains why steel is the ideal material for the Queensferry Crossing.

Charles Darwin's "Origin of Species", published in 1859, was hot off the press when steel first began to be used in bridge construction. Steel's potential for major civil engineering projects developed rapidly on both sides of the Atlantic from the middle of the 19th century onwards. Essentially an alloy of iron ore and carbon, this wonder material marked the end of wrought iron's domination as a construction material. Quite which bridge was the first to be built of steel is still disputed today, but certainly the Eads Bridge over the Mississippi River in Illinois, completed in 1874 and almost 2km in length, was one of the first significant bridges to use steel as its primary structural material.

In the UK, the Forth Bridge, which opened in 1890 after seven years construction, took the use of steel in global bridge construction to a new level. Today, it remains one of the most impressive feats of civil engineering anywhere in the world and, of course, instantly recognisable to millions of people. Next door, the Forth Road Bridge is made principally from steel and, at the time of its opening in 1964, featured the longest single bridge span in Europe.

Today, FCBC has the historic task of building another bridge across the Forth, this time a cable-stayed, as opposed to a suspension, bridge. Once again, steel is the main construction material being employed. Several key components of the new bridge are being fabricated in steel: these include the foundation caissons, the bridge deck and approach viaduct structures, the vehicle restraint system, the all-important stay cables and the anchor boxes which will secure the stay cables to the bridge's three towers, thereby connecting the towers to the bridge deck.

So, what makes steel the ideal material for our task? There are several features which make it unbeatable:

Strength & Weight First and foremost, steel is one of the strongest materials at the civil engineer's disposal but it is also relatively light. So it has a high strength-to-weight ratio which means that bridges can be built with inherent strength without being excessively heavy. Weight is usually the main enemy facing a bridge builder – unduly heavy bridges are rarely safe bridges. And lightweight construction techniques also bring cost benefits, not just in terms of construction but also cheaper transportation.

Durability & Versatility Steel is an incredibly resilient material capable of withstanding everything that extreme weather and climate conditions can throw at it. Steel bridges are commonly designed to have service lives of well over 100 years during which time degradation will be negligible. In addition, it is an extremely versatile material able to be shaped in any number of ways to create aesthetically pleasing end products. On top of this flexibility, steel has a tensile strength which allows it to be bent and pulled, perhaps as a result of strong buffeting from side winds. These features result in a product whose integrity and strength is easily maintained in complex and lengthy structures, whether vertical or horizontal. In short, it is ideal!

Reliability & Availability The combined effect of these properties is that steel is a thoroughly reliable material. Over the years, expertise in its use and capabilities has grown internationally to the extent that, today, it is the best understood construction material in the world. It is also readily available throughout the world, being manufactured in most industrial countries.

Speed of Construction A further advantage of the reduced weight of steel is that components can more easily be pre-fabricated off-site and transported to site ready to be installed.

Recyclable Finally, steel is recyclable. Indeed, it is the most recycled construction material in use today. When a steel bridge – or, for that matter, individual elements in it – reach the end of their useful life, the steel can be removed, cut into manageable sizes and returned to the steelworks to be melted down and re-used to manufacture new products.

For the technically minded, the grade of steel mostly used in the Queensferry Crossing is "S355J2 + N". This means it complies with the latest international quality construction standards. We are sourcing steel fabrications from a variety of countries including the UK, China, Poland and Spain. We are employing the latest, highly developed dehumidification and external coating techniques to ensure that the steel in the new bridge, especially in the cables, is protected from the damaging and corrosive effects of prolonged exposure to extreme weather conditions. Such corrosion on the existing Forth Road Bridge has, of course, been a factor in the decision to build a new bridge in the first place.

To summarise, steel is strong, light, versatile, durable, reliable, fast and environmentally responsible. What's not to like? There is no other material that can compare with steel, especially in the construction of large infrastructure projects such as the Queensferry Crossing. Its use is a thoroughly tried and tested technology, ideally suited to deliver a new major European bridge capable of meeting the demands that will be put upon it over the coming decades.

Below: Aerial view of deck sections lying in the dock storage area in October 2015. Some have had the top reinforced concrete deck installed and are ready to be taken out to the towers. Note the visiting cruise ship, a regular feature of summer life during bridge construction.

Left and below: One of the temporary steel trestles about to be installed on the Central Tower. These supported the weight of the initial four deck sections and temporary works platforms (see lower photo) positioned round each tower.

These casting operations took place both inside FCBC's dedicated 8,000 square metre Precast Production Sheds and later, after a decision to increase the rate of production, in the open air as well. Each deck section was transported to the casting areas using the SPMTs. Approximately 200 cubic metres of concrete from the neighbouring batching plant was poured into a shallow (minimum 250mm deep) slab covering each deck section and containing a double grid mat of heavy duty steel reinforcement bars (rebar). Once the concrete had reached sufficient strength, the deck was post-tensioned using lateral steel cables in order to provide extra stiffness, strength and stability in the structure. With the concrete deck in place, the average weight of each section had now increased to 750 tonnes (maximum 780 tonnes), still well within the capacity of the SPMTs.

At peak activity, the operations in the precast area in Rosyth Docks represented a major logistical challenge, perhaps best shown on the time-lapse videos posted on the Queensferry Crossing's YouTube channel [www.youtube.co.uk/queensferrycrossing] where the various manoeuvrings resemble an enormous game of chess with all the sections having to be moved about and

stored in the correct order ready for their next move.

A number of dockside tasks remained to be carried out before the deck section was ready to be taken out to the bridge site for installation. These included stripping out the temporary internal formwork used to create the support on which the reinforced concrete deck was cast and the first stage installation of the mechanical and electrical systems which would be so vital to the long term maintenance of the bridge once complete. Also installed at this stage were the fixings for the vehicle restraint system (better known as crash barriers) and the windshields as well as the drainage outlets and the guide pipes for the stay cable installation. Various temporary work components, designed to assist the lifting of each section as well as ensure the safety of all personnel working at height on the deck section during final installation, were also added.

Installation

During the summer of 2014, construction work out at the towers in mid estuary had reached above road deck height – 64m – roughly one third of their final, completed height. This triggered the start of work to prepare for the installation of the first deck sections. To enable this to happen, a huge amount of specially designed temporary steelwork – called "falsework" – totalling 7,200 tonnes was installed on each of the towers. The first elements to be erected were the series of six triangular falsework "trestles", 60m high and weighing 146 tonnes each, which were fixed to both sides of each tower from the top of the foundations to deck level. On top of them, temporary steel platforms were affixed (to a tolerance of just 50mm) which, in turn, supported the first pieces of permanent steel to be positioned on the bridge – the first deck sections themselves – which were lifted into place in September and October of that year. Another significant milestone for the Project. On each tower, the first four deck sections were fixed in place around the tower, in the case of the Central Tower by means of a complex "power joint" which is the only point along the entire length of the road deck where it is directly attached to the towers. At the North and South Towers, the deck is not fixed to the towers, thus allowing it to expand and contract and move according to temperature fluctuations, wind conditions and traffic load.

Lifting of the massive steel falsework and initial twelve deck sections (four per tower) was carried out by an enormous floating sheerleg crane with a lifting capacity at this high reach of 480 tonnes. Given that the deck sections emerging from the Precast Production Shed weighed up to

780 tonnes, it was necessary to save weight, so the three sets of four initial deck segments, weighing approximately 250 tonnes each, were lifted and installed without their reinforced concrete deck in place. Once welded and bolted together and resting on the falsework below, the reinforced concrete deck was cast in situ. When the towers had reached the requisite height to engage the first stay cables, these were attached to the initial deck sections and tensioned to set the deck to the vertical alignment required by the design. These first stay cables successfully took the weight of the deck for the first time in late August 2015, yet another key milestone for the Project.

Once the first deck sections were fixed in place but

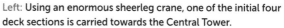

Left: **Using an enormous sheerleg crane, one of the initial four deck sections is carried towards the Central Tower.**

Top: **The blue 'erection travellers' under construction on land.**

Above: **Erection traveller hoists in position either side of a tower, ready to start lifting up the deck sections.**

before their concrete decks had been poured, the next operation was to lift up the six 250 tonne, blue "erection traveller" hoists which were set on rails bolted to the surface of the deck sections. These hydraulically powered cranes, one placed at either end of the emerging road deck cantilevers on all three towers, used a strand jack system to lift all subsequent deck sections into place from barges on the sea below. Fabricated in China, the erection travellers arrived on-site in four separate principal parts which were lifted on to the bridge structure by floating cranes and assembled in situ.

Cables

For many, the signature feature of the Queensferry Crossing – indeed, of all cable-stayed bridges – is the stay cable arrays which, fanning downwards from the towers

and catching the light in different ways at all times of the day, give the bridge its distinctive shape, appearance and character. It is the cables which, anchored at one end to the towers and, at the other, to the road deck, enable the towers to bear the immense load from the weight of the road deck, volume of traffic and wind forces.

In total, the Queensferry Crossing has 288 stay cables, the longest being 420m and the shortest 94m. Each cable consists of a varying number of strands (up to 109 for the largest cables) threaded through an external white pipe which acts essentially as a protective sleeve and controls the shape and hence the wind load on the cable. Every strand is made up of seven high tensile, galvanised steel wires, each 5.2 millimetres in diameter. Six of the wires, coated in wax, are wound in a helix pattern round a central king wire which is straight. The strands are individually

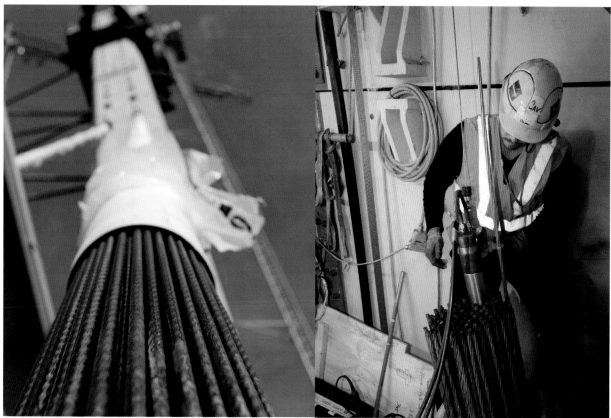

protected in a high density polyethylene (HDPE) sheath. In summary, seven wires equal one strand; a number of strands (between 45 and 109) equals one stay cable, 288 stay cables "equal" the Queensferry Crossing.

Out on the deck, individual lengths of external white pipe, also made of HDPE, were welded to the correct length for each individual cable. While laying stretched out on temporary cradles on the road deck, a single strand was threaded through. The pipe was now ready to be lifted into position using the tower crane. Once lifted and anchored at the top of the tower and inside the deck section down below, the remaining strands were then threaded through the pipe one by one using a winch and shuttle system. On completion of its threading, each individual strand was fed through holes in circular steel anchor plates and cut to length. At the lower level, these anchor plates were built into the steelwork of each deck section just beneath road level. At the upper level, they were built into a series of 4m high, 40 tonne steel anchor boxes stacked on top of each other inside the towers starting at a height of 150 metres. At both ends of each strand, a pair of small, conical, high tensile steel wedges locked the strands in position. Strands were individually tensioned as required up to a maximum of nine tonnes. The final result is one of the strongest steel cables in the world, easily capable of handling all loads likely to be imposed on the structure.

Top left: Multiple steel strands emerge from the white outer HDPE pipe during a cable installation operation on the South Tower.

Top right: Inside the anchor box high up in the North Tower, individual steel strands which make up the stay cables are wedged into position and tensioned.

Above: In September 2016, HRH The Duke of Edinburgh (seen here with FCBC Project Director, Michael Martin) paid a private site visit to be briefed on construction progress.

Left: **Required: a head for heights. Feeding the cable strands through the tower wall into the anchor boxes inside.**

Below: **Reels of steel cable strands wait on the bridge deck to be threaded inside the cable outer pipes.**

Opposite top left: **Small, high tensile steel wedges hold each cable strand in position in the anchor plate.**

Opposite top right: **Each incredibly strong cable strand consists of seven high tensile galvanised steel wires wrapped in a helix fashion before being wax coated and covered in a black HDPE sheath.**

Opposite middle: **A cable anchor plate with individual steel strands wedged firmly in place.**

Opposite below left: **At road deck level, cable strands pass through holes in the concrete deck before being secured in anchor plates beneath.**

Opposite below right: **Installing protective steel guide pipes at the lower – road deck - end of the cables.**

In total, the 288 stay cables on the Queensferry Crossing contain approximately 6,300 tonnes of high tensile steel wire which, if joined together, would measure 23,000 miles, almost enough to stretch right around the world.

Road deck construction

During the second half of 2014 and the first half of 2015, construction work continued on the towers in mid estuary and, on land, the casting of the reinforced concrete decks on each road deck section. By September 2015, the construction team was ready to start lifting the remaining 110 deck sections into place, a process that would last through to February 2017.

For each deck section, the first stage of the journey was to transport it to the appropriate tower. The sections were firstly loaded on to barges at the quayside where they had been initially off-loaded several months previously. A SPMT carried each deck section on to the barge which was equipped with powerful ballasting mechanisms which allowed it to maintain a constant level in the water despite the average 750 tonne load arriving on its deck. FCBC deployed two barges, the larger being capable of carrying two deck sections at a time – approximately 1,500 tonnes.

The barge was then towed out into the Forth by tugs. On arrival at the tower, the barge was anchored - to within a tight 200mm tolerance with the help of GPS – beneath the blue erection traveller cranes up on the road deck cantilevers, one at either end . A single, four-point lifting tackle was next lowered from the erection traveller and attached to the deck section. Once final inspections had been completed and assuming favourable wind and tidal conditions, the lifting operation could begin using the erection traveller's twin 580 tonne hydraulic strand jacks.

Deck sections, mounted on barges, making their way to the towers.

A deck section is loaded on to a barge in the dockyard, a delicate operation.

Top: The blue lifting tackle is attached to the deck section in preparation for beginning the lifting operation.

Above: Lift-off! The deck section begins its journey 60 metres into the air.

As the strand jacks took the load and the deck section slowly began to rise in 1m strokes of the jack, the barge, controlled by its ballasting mechanisms, rose with the deck, thus minimising the risk of pitching and consequent possible collision with the deck section. As the deck continued to rise, so the barge was able to be moved out of the way and the deck section, suspended in mid-air, could continue upwards towards its final position.

Typically, it took around four hours to lift a deck section up to road deck height of up to 60m. On arrival at deck height, the section would be offset by some 200mm from the previously installed deck section. Smaller jacks now pulled the section in to interlock with the flange plates of the previous unit. The newly arrived section was tilted by a few degrees to match the final geometry of the completed bridge deck and the series of interlocking plates were bolted together to hold the new arrival in its final position. A strict 2mm accuracy was needed to align adjacent deck sections so that the process of installing the 1,600 bolts per section would go smoothly. That this operation went almost faultlessly throughout the deck erection process was testimony to the benefits of the trial assembly back in Shanghai as well as the expertise of the CSB (Cable-Stayed Bridge) team on-site.

Once the section had been correctly positioned, it had to be fixed permanently in place. This was achieved by

Left: After further checks that all is well, the lift operation continues...

Below: ... the deck section being slowly lifted higher and higher by the erection traveller hoist...

Above: ... in an operation which typically takes up to four hours...

Left: ...until it reaches its destination, 60 metres up, and arrives next to the previously lifted deck section.

plates in the deck section and in the tower. Each deck section has two dedicated, permanent cables descending in parallel from the tower. Initially, even once the cables had been fully assembled and anchored, the weight of the deck section was still primarily being carried by the erection traveller sitting on the previously installed deck section. Only once the cables had been tensioned up to their calculated load could the installation of the deck section be declared complete and the full weight of the deck section be transferred from the erection traveller to the cables themselves.

Next, the lifting tackle was disconnected and hydraulic jacks launched the erection traveller forward on its rails in between the just installed and fully tensioned cables to the leading edge of the newly installed deck section and made ready to lift the next deck section making its way out from the dock. And so the cycle was repeated with every step in the sequence having to be fully completed before the next could begin. A typical cycle time was two weeks with the best achieved being nine days.

The construction team was amused on 1st April 2015 – note the date - when a Scottish daily newspaper carried a

welding right around the steel box structure and the internal strengthening longitudinal beams inside. This was a time-consuming operation but a critical one as a flawless top flange was vital to allow a 750mm wide reinforced concrete "stitch" to be poured along the seam of the two, now-joined deck sections, thus creating a continuous deck slab. These operations were constantly monitored by a team of inspectors to ensure perfect positioning was achieved.

At this point, the stay cables were prepared, lifted into position and anchored, top and bottom, to the anchor

QUEENSFERRY P E O P L E

Florian Dieterle

More Scottish weather

In an article which appeared in the July 2016 edition of the Queensferry Crossing Project Update newsletter, Florian Dieterle, FCBC's Cable-Stayed Bridge Temporary Works Co-ordinator, looks at the challenges posed by the Scottish weather when lifting such huge structures.

Since September last year, FCBC has successfully lifted 80 deck sections from sea level to road deck level on the Queensferry Crossing. Each lift operation is a major civil engineering feat in its own right. Remember, the structures we are lifting weigh on average around 750 tonnes (or roughly 54 London buses – with passengers!), they measure 40m by 16m by 4m (so they're big!) and we have to lift them up an incredible 60m (200ft) into the air! To top it all, we are carrying out these operations in the middle of a wide, exposed, maritime estuary. This is tough civil engineering!

It's a huge challenge and, every day, we face a number of significant variables which govern how well each lift will go and how long it will take. These variables are mostly weather related and, in Scotland, there is never any shortage of weather!

Let's start with wind. We cannot begin lifting such huge structures in wind conditions over 21 knots (or 11m per second). Wind can cause the road deck, on which the blue "erection traveller" crane is situated, to move, albeit fractionally, just as it is designed to do. This could

have knock-on effects on the movement of the deck section once it becomes airborne making precise control difficult. That's why we liaise very closely with the Met Office to identify suitable windows of opportunity where we can be confident of being able to start and complete a lift operation in safe, low wind conditions.

Wind also affects when we can lift the main stay cable pipes into position. If we cannot finish and fully tension the cables supporting the previously installed deck section, then we cannot move the erection traveller forwards and, consequently, cannot start the next deck lift. Our operations out there are sequential. One stage has to be fully completed before the next can begin. If wind delays the completion of one operation, then subsequent operations will also be delayed. And, when it comes to wind, there's nothing we can do about it. Not out in the middle of the Forth.

Frustratingly, days can sometimes be lost waiting for the right wind conditions. Even in May this year, when the country experienced three or four consecutive weeks of warm, sunny weather, we lost some working days due to continuing variable and blustery wind conditions out on the Forth.

Then there's fog. As local residents will testify, the Forth Estuary is prone to mist and fog, known locally on the east coast of Scotland as "haar". Good visibility is vital so that the barge carrying the deck section can sail out from the dock to the tower site and to allow us to start the lift operation itself. For safety's sake, we have to be able to see every part of the operation. Powerful floodlighting means that, if necessary, we can perform a lift in reduced light conditions just as well as during the day. This is particularly important in the winter months with their shorter days.

Sea conditions are also important to a successful and timely deck lift. We can lift in both falling and rising tides, but waves of over 0.3m (1ft) in height can result in movements in the barge which could affect the way the deck section begins its journey upwards. So we pause to wait for the waves to subside. Waves, of course, are largely a result of wind and a 1ft wave out on the Forth, as sailors out of Port Edgar will tell you, is a very common thing. So wind, fog and waves are the main "enemy". Other meteorological conditions, such as rain, snow, severe cold, frost or even a sudden heatwave, pose less of a challenge in themselves, though they may bring some obvious safety considerations for staff. We don't necessarily object to bad weather: we just hope it happens in the middle of the night, thus leaving us to get on with our day jobs unhindered.

Above: **Back in the office, members of the CSB (Cable-Stayed Bridge) team meet with planning colleagues to review deck lifting progress.**

news story claiming that FCBC had not ordered enough steel and that, consequently, the new bridge would be left with a permanent 18 inch gap in the middle of the road deck. To overcome this hurdle, the article claimed that vehicles would have to accelerate over a ramp in order to clear the gap!

Weather considerations

As was only to be expected in such an exposed location as the Firth of Forth, certain weather conditions had to prevail before a deck lift operation could get underway. As far as wind - the main challenge at all times - was concerned, Met Office forecasts had to be predicting a four-hour weather window at sea level where wind speed would not exceed 11m per second (approximately 25 mph). Once underway, that figure could rise to 14m per second (approximately 31 mph). Initially, the team preferred to start a lift on a rising tide which helped minimise any risk of damage to either deck section or barge at lift-off. Over time, however, with the team's experience growing as a series of deck lifts were successfully completed, this became less of a consideration. Similarly, in the early days the team preferred to carry out lifts in daylight hours but with experience this also became less important and the shorter days during the winter months presented no

additional problems. Experience gained on the job meant lifts would take place at any time of the day or night as necessary, seven days a week.

The Firth of Forth is prone to frequent mists, especially during the spring and autumn. On occasion, this did delay the start of some lifts, good visibility being vital not only to the preparations and early stages of each lift but also the safe manoeuvring of marine traffic. The importance of advance planning, accurate forecasts and precisely executed preparations was brought home daily to those involved in making things happen. Once any lift was underway, it had to be completed no matter what changes in the weather might occur, so correct preparation and careful study of the weather forecasts were vital.

Balanced cantilever construction method and a Guinness World Record

The Queensferry Crossing's road deck was built using the balanced cantilever construction method by which deck sections were installed one at a time on alternate sides of each tower, thus creating a balance in the growing cantilevers on either side as subsequent deck sections were

Top left and top right: **With the deck section in position, welding could begin around the entire perimeter to join it to its neighbour.**

Above right: **Deck lifting operations sometimes had to take place in less than ideal visibility.**

Above left: **Once the deck section has been joined to the road deck and the stay cables installed, the lifting tackle can be removed and the cycle begins again with the next deck section.**

Opposite page top: **A striking view of one of the internal walkways – stretching 2.7km end to end - inside the bridge's road deck.**

Opposite page bottom: **As the emerging road deck became ever longer, so the amount of deflection caused by successive deck section lifts became ever greater, here reaching a maximum of about 4 metres.**

added. Once again, this echoed the construction technique of its neighbour, the Forth Bridge, in the 1880s, showing that fundamental engineering principles never change. Obviously, as one deck section was lifted up, the cantilever structure would deflect down noticeably on that side, before having the equilibrium restored with the next lift on the opposite side. In order to minimise this increasing effect as the cantilevers grew outwards, temporary tie-down cables were installed connecting the bottom of each tower to the underside of the emerging road deck, thus reducing the degree of deflection on the opposite side and reducing the strain on the base of the towers.

In October 2016, the free-standing Central Tower span – the sum of the length of the two cantilevers attached to the Tower – reached its maximum length of 644 metres. After a thorough inspection and endorsement by independent civil engineers, this unique structure, constructed from 36 separate steel and concrete composite deck sections, was officially recognised by Guinness World Records as the longest, free-standing, balanced cantilever structure ever built anywhere in the world. This recognition of the feats of engineering being achieved on the Queensferry Crossing was the cause of much celebration and supports the widely held view that this bridge is a special structure in which current and future generations will take great pride (see photos on page 111).

The normal sequence of lifting deck sections one after the other had to be varied when it came to installing the sections which sit on top of Piers S1 and S2. The blue

Above: **Another successful deck lift completed – though you wouldn't know it from the shore!**

Right: **Temperature inversions out on the Forth gave rise to some spectacular photos, in this case the South Tower taken from the top of the Central Tower.**

erection traveller hoists which had the job of lifting up the sections had only a ltd horizontal reach. Lifting sections in sequence right up to the piers would have meant having to reach out some distance over the top of the pier structure in order to lift the next - pier-top - section. Instead, the pier-top sections were lifted up "ahead of time" and, once at full height, were slid out forwards on bearings fixed on top of the piers. Whilst it may have looked to the casual observer that it was balancing precariously on top of the tower, the section was, of course, firmly secured in position. The next task was to lift up another section to fill the gap left between the pier and the emerging road deck and then join them together as normal.

On any bridge project, large or small, the moment when the gap is finally "bridged" or closed is a significant milestone. There were four principal closures on the Queensferry Crossing, the first being achieved in July 2016 when the North Tower span was joined to the northern approach viaduct. The others were: the North Tower deck span to the Central Tower deck span; the Central Tower deck span to the South Tower deck span and, finally in

February 2017, the South Tower deck span to the southern approach viaduct.

By October 2016, at the point when the Central Tower span was receiving its few minutes of fame in the international spotlight, the gaps between the span and its neighbours on the North and South Towers had narrowed to a matter of just six metres and only two more deck sections – the smaller closure pieces – remained to be lifted into position, one on either side. These closure sections (measuring 6.1m by 39.8m by 4.9m) nevertheless still weighed a very considerable 300 tonnes. The operation to lift these sections into place was technically extremely challenging not least because, with only small clearances on either side, there was no room for error. Complete

This page: Cause for celebration: in October 2016, the 644 metre long Central Tower span is officially recognised by Guinness World Records as the longest, free-standing, balanced cantilever structure ever built. A tremendous achievement.

accuracy during these lifts would be even more vital than ever.

In order to maximise the available gap, the entire South Tower deck span was pushed back 300mm using powerful 400 tonne hydraulic jacks attached to the Tower itself. This created a space sufficiently wide to allow the closure section to slip into place without a hitch.

The next step was to join the newly arrived section to the South Tower span in much the same way as all the previous deck sections had been installed – by welding it

into place before pouring a reinforced concrete stitch across the top of the join to create the final deck surface on which the road surfacing would be laid. Unlike other deck sections, closure pieces were not bolted into place but a series of temporary tension bars, called Macalloy bars, pulled the two decks tightly together allowing the welding operation to take place.

Once the section was fully attached on one side to the South Tower deck span, preparations were made to attach the other end to the Central Tower span. Before that could take place, however, checks on the horizontal and vertical alignments had to be made to ensure an exact match. Vertical differences between the two cantilevered decks could reach a maximum of 4m depending on wind conditions. At the point when a closure is set to be achieved, the cantilevers have reached, by definition, their greatest length and, consequently, deflections will be maximised. By altering the tension on the cables supporting the already installed deck sections, the leading edges of the two sections to be joined were minutely adjusted to the correct geometry. A temporary steel frame containing small adjustment jacks was laid across the gap between the two cantilevers in order to stabilise any movement and reduce it to zero.

For each closure, this final adjustment process also included an operation known as "green cutting" which was carried out on land before the closure deck section was taken out to be installed. Out on the bridge deck, precise final measurements were taken of the remaining gap to be closed. The leading edge of the steel section, which was originally fabricated a fraction too large in order to cater for any small variance at this critical juncture, was trimmed back by a few millimetres, using oxyacetylene cutters, to ensure a 100% accurate fit out on-site and to allow a perfect weld to be formed between the section and its neighbour.

When everything was ready to everyone's satisfaction, the compression on the hydraulic jacks holding the South Tower span back was slowly released so that the entire 690m structure could move back the 300mm, thus closing the gap. The other side of the closure section could now be welded and concreted into positon – and full closure achieved. In all, closure operations took an average of two weeks each to complete.

The historic, final deck lift took place on 3rd February 2017 and the final closure, when the South Tower span was connected to the southern approach viaduct, followed on 1st March. The basic structure of the new bridge was now complete but there remained many tasks to carry out

Opposite page: **Another deck section nears its destination on the South Tower span. Note the deck section installed in advance on top of Pier S1 (see page 108 for explanation).**

Left: **Looking down from road deck level as another deck section – this time one of the smaller closure sections - is lifted up in November 2016.**

Above: **Deck lifting operations were carried out 24 hours a day, weather conditions allowing.**

before the bridge itself could be declared finished and ready to open to traffic.

Cable Crossover

A particular feature of the Queensferry Crossing's aesthetic elegance is the highly visible overlapping stay-cables covering 140m lengths of the road deck where the flanking North and South Tower cable fans meet the Central Tower fan. This is not for visual impact: these crossover cables are an innovative solution to the challenge of stabilising the middle tower in any three-tower, cable-stayed bridge.

The North and South Towers are stabilised primarily by back-span cables anchored directly over V-shaped piers beneath the northern and southern approach viaducts. The reinforced concrete Piers N1 and S1 prevent the deck from lifting up by the installation of six stressed tie-down cables fed through the hollow pier legs from deck to anchor points fixed in the piers' foundations. But, being situated alone in mid-estuary with no direct link to the approach viaduct piers, no such stabilisation was possible for the Central Tower, standing secure, by gravity, on its foundations on Beamer Rock.

This is the reason for the use of ten overlapping stay

cables in each of the two main spans. These have the effect of doubling – to four in number – the cable supports to each of the ten mid-span deck sections both sides of the Central Tower. The stiffening provided by these overlapping cables increases the effective structural depth of the deck at mid-span in the form of a virtual truss. This stiffens the entire structure sufficient for it to stabilise the Central Tower, allowing the three towers to share the same slender, tapering profile.

These overlapping cables contain fewer strands than found in other cables and demanded a complex sequence of stress adjustment in the nearby main cables. The longest cables on the Queensferry Crossing, at 420m, are the longest crossover cables.

The last lap – final pieces of the jigsaw

With the bridge structure complete, the construction team entered the final phase of the works which would see the entire Project finished and ready for opening to traffic in August 2017. It was perhaps not readily appreciated by casual observers, but the scale of late-stage activities to be completed before a bridge such as the Queensferry Crossing can be declared open to traffic was enormous and the list extensive.

Left: Closing the gap: the closure deck section between the Central and South Tower spans slots neatly into place in October 2016.

Middle: A close up view of a deck section approaching the end of its upwards journey.

Lower: 3rd February 2017, the final piece of the jigsaw, the last closure deck section arrives in position between the South Tower span and the south approach viaduct.

Tower cranes

From the passer-by's point of view, the most obvious activity was the dismantling and removal of the three huge, yellow tower cranes which, having arrived on-site in 2013 and having been built to a height of just over 235m, had become very familiar landmarks. They had dominated the skyline and had performed their tasks magnificently over the years. In fact, many people were sorry to see them eventually come down, inevitable though it was. With a combined weight of approximately 1,400 tonnes, their removal was a major task. The dismantling of these monsters was carried out by a reversal of the process which saw them go up in the first place. Each section of the

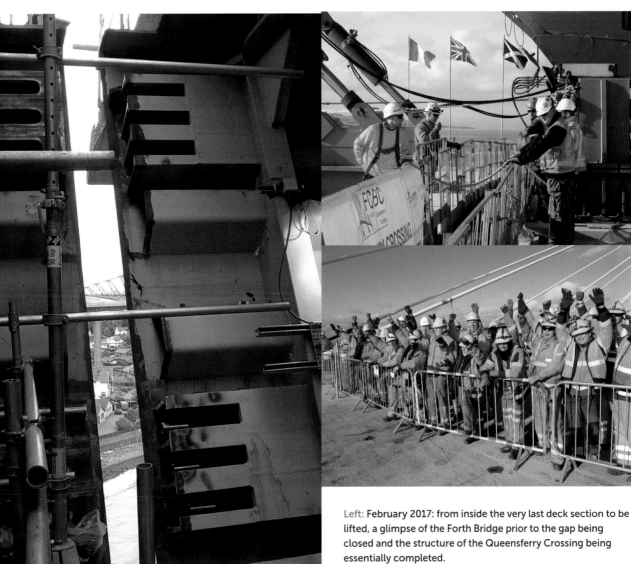

Left: **February 2017: from inside the very last deck section to be lifted, a glimpse of the Forth Bridge prior to the gap being closed and the structure of the Queensferry Crossing being essentially completed.**

Top: **After 122 deck lifts, the final deck section makes its way into position.**

Above: **The deck team celebrating the successful completion of the final deck lift.**

crane's mast structure was removed by the crane's own jib and lowered to the ground while the crane's weight is temporarily borne by a separate hydraulically operated external climbing frame. However, a key difference between the installation and removal of the tower cranes was that, during installation, the horizontal jib section of the crane was always above the height of the growing tower and was free to rotate 360 degrees allowing it to "weathervane" in strong winds. In the dismantling process, the jib had to remain in a fixed position parallel to the bridge deck below since it could not rotate due to the proximity of the tower structure and stay-cables.

This meant that a weather window of low wind levels for two consecutive days was necessary to allow any dismantling to proceed. Prior to the removal of each tower crane, smaller temporary gantry cranes were installed at the top of each tower to lift the final stay-cables into place and handle any necessary final lifts of materials. These gantry cranes were designed to be dismantled into small enough pieces to be removed inside the tower after these operations were complete.

Temporary formwork

The tower-top temporary formwork structures – the "birdcages" – had all been removed by autumn 2016. The other temporary steel formwork, such as the trestles and

Above: Its job done, the North Tower jump form is lifted clear of the tower top and is lowered to the ground.

platforms beneath each of the road deck spans, were dismantled and removed during the spring 2017. Like the tower cranes, the removal of such large and heavy pieces of engineering hardware was a significant and complicated task in its own right. Bit by bit, the final unadorned appearance of the new bridge was being revealed.

Temporary caissons

The dismantling of the tower cranes and falsework was the trigger for the removal of the two remaining 11m high temporary caissons which had been attached to the permanent caissons ever since they were positioned on the seabed in 2013. These temporary extensions had kept the rim of the caissons above water level, thus creating and maintaining dry internal conditions in which the reinforced concrete tower foundations could be laid. They had also acted as a "quayside" alongside which the service barges for the North and South Towers and Pier S1 could be moored throughout the construction programme.

The temporary caissons – and the Beamer Rock cofferdam for the Central Tower - were cut away and removed in sections, for the first time allowing the sea to lap up against the base of the towers as the design intended.

Beamer rock reinstatement

To properly apply the finishing touches to Beamer Rock, dolerite excavated from the Whinnyhill rock cut north of the Queensferry Crossing was shipped out and used to dress the tower base, thus returning the Rock to its original appearance.

Mechanical, electrical and plumbing

Among other items to be installed at this stage were the mechanical, electrical and plumbing (MEP) works. Primarily, this involved the installation of the electrical systems needed to power the main carriageway bollard lighting on the approach viaducts, the architectural up-lighting and down-lighting on the outside of the bridge structure and the over-carriageway sign and ITS gantries as well as marine and aviation navigation warning lights. Contained within the deck and towers are the interior lighting, the dehumidification systems, the structural health monitoring system, the fire detection and protection system and the maintenance shuttle and lift cars, all of which need power. Some of the infrastructure and ducting required for these electrical systems was installed in modular fashion inside each deck section back on land before they were lifted into position on the bridge. Also to be installed were the fibre optics and electrical wiring connecting the bridge's operating systems to the Forth Bridges Control Room two

Above: **One of 12 panels which made up the South Tower's temporary caisson being removed in August 2017, allowing the sea to flow in against the Tower's wall.**

Right: **The final section of the Central Tower's foundation cofferdam being removed prior to the reinstatement of the Beamer Rock surface.**

kilometres away in South Queensferry. Finally, lightning conductors were installed at the top of the three towers.

The daily operation of the Queensferry Crossing and the health of the entire structure require a comprehensive, state-of-the-art system of monitoring carried out by a range of sensors placed at strategic locations. Wind, temperature, rainfall and general weather conditions are monitored 24 hours a day through sensors placed at road deck level and on top of the towers. 34 accelerometers measure the rate of movement of the principal structural elements in order to gauge the lateral, vertical, longitudinal and torsional acceleration and velocity of the bridge movements. Strain gauges constantly measure the strain being experienced by individual strands within the cables caused by the load they are being asked to carry principally on the road deck but also due to temperature and weather variations.

All of the items requiring power also had to be installed on or in the bridge structure. Although sometimes described as "finishing touches", in fact they each represent a major construction task in themselves and are a vital ingredient in the safe and efficient long term performance of the Queensferry Crossing.

Cable guide pipes and dampers

In order to prevent any potential damage to the stay cables at the point where they enter through the reinforced concrete deck just above their anchor plates, angled steel guide pipes were placed around the lower end of all 288 cables. These guide pipes also act as the housing for cable dampers. These dampers act as energy dissipating devices to stop damaging vibrations of the cables occurring. The mechanism uses friction generated by spring loaded pads which control the tendency of the cables to oscillate in particular wind conditions, movements which, over time, could lead to fatigue and compromise the strength and effectiveness of the individual steel strands which make up the cable.

Above: Spring 2017, with the road deck structure complete and the stay cables fully tensioned, the temporary support trestles could be removed for recycling.

Inspection gantries and cradles

In order to allow regular inspections and maintenance of the towers, approach viaducts, road deck and cables, a number of gantries and cradles had to be installed on the bridge structure. These include four mobile gantries beneath the road deck and a further two beneath the viaducts. In addition, climbing gantries can be affixed to the stay cables in order to carry out close quarter inspection of the entire length of each cable. Similarly, cradles attached to ropes fixed to the sides of the towers allow for inspection of the exteriors of the tower walls.

Waterproofing

On the road deck, the finished blacktop road surface had to be laid on both carriageways, 2.7km from the north to south abutments. First of all, the full length of the reinforced concrete deck over each road deck section was cleared and cleaned in preparation for the application of a waterproofing membrane. Concrete can deteriorate, over time, through water ingress, particularly in an environment like the Forth Estuary where water-borne salts can corrode the steel reinforcement. Concrete decks are especially vulnerable as they are exposed to high volumes of rain water.

It was, therefore, necessary to protect the concrete in these areas from water. This was achieved by applying a highly durable waterproof membrane directly on to the concrete surface. A minimum of two 2mm layers was required producing a polymer membrane designed to last at least 50 years. Any rainwater making its way through the surface "blacktop" meets the waterproofing and is shed harmlessly into drains built into either side of the carriageway.

Waterproofing is a hidden, yet absolutely vital, measure to ensure the long-term viability of the Queensferry Crossing and its associated approach structures.

124

Road surface

The road surfacing was laid in three layers to provide a minimum thickness of 130mm. Firstly, an Additional Protection Layer of hot rolled asphalt, nominally 45mm thick, was placed directly on top of the waterproofing before a second, Binder Course layer, nominally 50mm thick, was overlaid. Finally, a 35mm layer of low noise surface course (Transport Scotland's innovative TS2010 specification thin surfacing) was laid in an operation known as "echelon paving" where three road pavers lay the surfacing simultaneously, thereby eliminating any longitudinal joints on the top surface. The road surface was laid to the highest possible standard, ensuring a consistent,

Top left and right: Once the reinforced concrete was poured to form the road deck and before the final road surface is laid, two layers of waterproofing membranes are sprayed over the entire surface area to provide long-term protection against rain and water-borne salts.

Above: Each tower hosts a pair of sign gantries to provide vital, up-to-the-minute information to drivers. Here, the northbound sign gantry is installed on the North Tower.

Above: Diagram showing the composition of the final road surface over which traffic passes.

high quality finish not only on the bridge itself but extending beyond into the new motorway works.

Windshielding

Wind can have a significant effect on traffic flow and safety as vehicles cross the bridge in stormy conditions. This has been demonstrated several times over the years by adverse events on the Forth Road Bridge. That's why the Queensferry Crossing incorporates a modern, high performance windshielding system designed to protect vehicles from the worst effects of the wind.

With their top rails 3.6m higher than the road surface, windshielding panels run the full length of the bridge and

approach viaducts and as far as the west side of the Ferrytoll Viaduct north of the Queensferry Crossing. Featuring parallel open louvres held in place by galvanised steel posts and rails, these panels break up the wind and deflect it upwards over the road deck, reducing the overturning moment on high-sided vehicles by approximately 50% and creating a relatively low-wind environment in which vehicles can travel safely. The louvres are made of a high quality, transparent acrylic material resistant to harmful ultraviolet (UV) rays from the sun and laced with polymer strips to alert birdlife to their presence. The transparency results in good visibility so that motorists can enjoy the views as they cross the bridge.

The Queensferry Crossing's windshielding system is designed to ensure that the bridge can stay open to traffic even in extreme winds of up to 115mph. An added benefit is the architectural floodlighting incorporated into the windshields, which outlines the elegant curved shape of the road deck when viewed from the shore at night. On the first 200m of the southern approach viaduct, PVC infills create a solid barrier to help mitigate the effects of traffic noise on nearby residents.

Expansion joints

Movement is a feature which must be considered in the design of all structures. In the case of bridges such as the Queensferry Crossing, movements can be vertical, longitudinal and lateral. Anyone who has ever walked across the Forth Road Bridge will have felt the mostly vertical movement of the walkway beneath their feet. The

Left and above: Expansion joints at both ends of the north and southbound carriageways enable the bridge to move vertically, longitudinally and laterally according to ambient temperature, traffic volume and wind load.

ability to move helps bridges cope with the weather-related and traffic loading demands they face every day.

There are three principal causes of movement:

- Temperature: steel and concrete structures expand in heat and contract in cold conditions
- Traffic: the more traffic on the bridge, the greater the vertical load on the structure
- Wind: the higher the wind, the greater the lateral load on the structure

Expansion joints incorporated into the structure allow these constant movements to take place without damaging the bridge. On the Queensferry Crossing, four expansion joints (two each for both north and southbound carriageways) are situated 2.7km apart at the north and south abutments. Constructed from steel and rubber, they expand and contract with the longitudinal movement of the bridge and are designed, in the most extreme conditions, to accommodate a movement of 1.7m at the north abutment and 2.4m at the south abutment. They feature specially designed interlocking top plates (called "sinus" plates) which reduce tyre noise generated by vehicles by up to 80% and also provide a smooth ride for traffic.

Above: Many complex electrical systems control the functioning of the bridge. Here, technicians finalise the installation of one of the main electricity switchboards in the south abutment.

Paint

Just as with its distinctive 19th century neighbour, the Forth Bridge, paint plays an important role in the appearance of the Queensferry Crossing which, given that an amazing total of 600,000 litres were used, is hardly surprising. The external and internal surfaces of the main road deck and viaduct sections were painted at the fabricators' yards prior to being delivered to site. A four-coat system was used comprising, firstly, a zinc primer followed by two coats of micaceous iron oxide undercoat and a final top coat of semi-gloss paint in a shade called "Goose Grey". Out on the Forth, the only areas of painting required to be carried out were principally round the joins between deck sections and, in the last phase of the construction programme, to fill in small areas where temporary items of formwork - gantries and support brackets, for example - had been affixed to the steel super-structure. The paint has an expected durability of 20 years before any significant maintenance will be required.

Above: **The bridge's final road surface is created in an operation called 'echelon paving': a thin layer of low-noise asphalt is simultaneously laid across the two motorway lanes and the hard shoulder to achieve a totally smooth surface without joints.**

Viaducts

With some justification, a lay person would probably define a cable-stayed bridge such as the Queensferry Crossing as the entire length of built structure lying between the two abutments where the road deck meets terra firma on either shore. Civil engineers, however, would define things differently. To them, a cable-stayed bridge is only that part of the overall structure which, lying out in the middle of the estuary, is supported by the cables anchored to the towers.

In other words, the bridge structure itself does not reach land at all. Instead, the gap between the two is filled by approach viaducts whose principal function is to span shallow water and connect the bridge to the approach roads on land. Supported from beneath on a series of piers, the viaducts differ from the main road deck which is supported from above by the stay cables. The engineering methods adopted to build and position the viaducts are quite unlike those used to erect the road deck on the bridge. However, there are also a number of similarities in the way their road deck sections were put together.

Chapter 4 looked at the design and construction of the foundations of the Queensferry Crossing's northern and southern approach viaducts. The focus here is on how the construction team assembled the viaducts and launched them into position. The main difference between the construction methods used to build the viaducts and the bridge's road deck arises from the fact that the viaducts are situated in shallow water nearer the north and south shores of the Forth Estuary and are, therefore, inaccessible by barge. This meant that lifting the separate sections up from barges on the water would be impossible. Instead, the basic structures of both approach viaducts would have to be pre-assembled on land and launched out incrementally over the supporting piers.

Approach Viaduct South (AVS) fabrication

The most notable feature of the AVS was that it was constructed of two separate lengths of steel box girders, trapezoidal in cross-section, one carrying the northbound carriageway, the other the southbound. In total, the resulting twin box deck section viaduct was 543m long and the steelwork weighed 7,000 tonnes (without the reinforced concrete deck).

Similar to the cable-stayed road deck across the bridge, both carriageways were constructed in sections, 19 each. The sections, weighing an average of 130 tonnes and 28.4m in length, were fabricated off-site in Darlington by Cleveland Bridge UK. Arriving in two longitudinal halves ready to be welded together, deliveries to site - by lorry - began in the autumn of 2013.

On-site preparation

On arrival, the sections were off-loaded and temporarily stored on cleared ground beyond the south abutment, ground that would, on completion of the entire Project, carry the main carriageway of the realigned A90, the main trunk road to and from Edinburgh. This ground was known as the Launching Bay. Manoeuvring the separate sections around the site as necessary was facilitated by a specially designed overhead gantry crane with a 140 tonne capacity. This same crane was later dismantled, transported across the Forth Road Bridge and reassembled on the construction-site of the northern approach viaduct to perform the same function. Once on-site, the sections were welded and bolted together to create separate lengths ready for launch. The accurate alignment of the sections as they were welded together was absolutely critical.

Incremental launch

Once two sections had been welded together end-on, the combined structure was ready to be launched out towards the first piers. This was done by attaching them via steel cables to twin 500 tonne capacity hydraulic strand jacks attached to the south abutment. This system was capable of moving the sections horizontally on bearings at a speed of about 6m per hour, typically 90m at a time. In order to overcome any downward gravitational deflection of the leading edge as the section made its way forwards between piers – a span of 87m – 35m high steel "king posts" were installed 85m back from the leading edge. Cables attached to these king posts, stressed up to 450 tonnes by means of jacks at the rear, lifted the front edge of the structure to create sufficient clearance to meet lateral guides positioned on top of each completed pier, effectively making it a miniature cable-stayed bridge at this stage. These guides, featuring a series of greased, flat-plate, Teflon-coated bearings, ensured that the viaduct steel sections were always in exactly the right alignment as they continued their journey out towards the cable-stayed bridge. The first launch took place in December 2013.

Construction of the deeper water piers furthest away from the south abutment continued while the early stages of the AVS launch got underway.

In total, there were six such launches for each carriageway on the AVS, a process that took 18 months to complete. Starting its launch phase before any road deck sections were installed out at the bridge's towers, the AVS was, in fact, the first stretch of constructed deck on the Queensferry Crossing. The launch of the AVS carriageways started in the autumn of 2013 and proceeded through the following year, finally being completed in June 2015.

Launching such a vast structure – 7,000 tonnes of steel, more than 500m in length, over six piers, working at height – was a significant civil engineering achievement.

AVS – reinforced concrete deck and closure

Once the AVS had reached its final position, the in-situ laying of the reinforced concrete deck along the length of both carriageways could get underway. This is the structure on which the final road surface is laid which will carry traffic to and from the bridge. Due to weight considerations, it was not possible to launch the viaduct with its concrete decks already installed. In a process similar to that used to lay the reinforced concrete deck across the individual deck sections in the dockside Precast Sheds, internal scaffolding and shuttering were first installed, section by section, on top of which two layers of heavy duty steel reinforcement bars were laid followed by the pouring of concrete to create a 250mm thick deck slab. This took the average weight of each section up to 600 tonnes. The work was carried out over seven phases, the first six being completed by the middle of 2016 while the final phase was able to be completed only in April 2017 after the lifting into place of the final road deck section between the South Tower span and the AVS and the pulling shut of the remaining 400mm gap between that final section and the AVS. This involved using strand jacks to pull first the northbound, then the southbound carriageways forwards by the required distance, each weighing 10,000 tonnes.

This closure marked a very significant milestone in the construction of the Queensferry Crossing, the completion of the entire structure from shore to shore.

Approach Viaduct North (AVN) fabrication

The structure and scale of the northern approach viaduct differed from its southern counterpart in many ways. First of all, at 222m in length, it was more than 50% shorter. And at approximately 5,000 tonnes of steel, it was

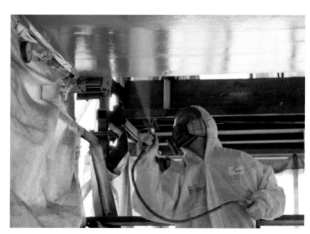

Above: Painting another Forth bridge: a total of 600,000 litres of protective paint was applied to the external and internal surfaces of the deck sections.

Above: Looking north through the Approach Viaduct South's eight reinforced concrete support piers.

also significantly lighter. In terms of construction on-site, however, there were similarities between the two in that the AVN was assembled in trapezoidal sections, welded and bolted together on dry land just to the north of the north abutment. Again, shallow water and rocks close in to shore on the north side of the estuary meant the sections could not be conventionally lifted from a barge by erection traveller hoist. Besides, part of the AVN is permanently situated over dry land. Coupled with a steep cliff bank and marine environmental considerations, construction of the viaduct on land and a land-based launch was the preferred solution.

The structure of the AVN differed significantly from the AVS. The AVN comprised a length of two separate box girders, one for the northbound and one for southbound

carriageway (similar to the AVS) made from eight twin box sections. This stretch measured 76m in length and was situated at the north end of the viaduct structure. At its southern edge, it was connected to a 146m length of 12 single, full width box girders similar in structure to the main crossing's road deck sections. In fact, once the Queensferry Crossing structure was complete, this stretch of the AVN became an integrated part of the main crossing road deck supported by stay cables. But, being unable to be lifted into place in the traditional way due to shallow in-shore water, it had to be constructed and launched as part of the AVN.

The twin box sections of the AVN super-structure were fabricated by Cleveland Bridge UK who had also fabricated the AVS sections. ZPMC in China, who fabricated the main crossing's road deck sections, fabricated the larger single box sections which were delivered in "flat pack" form for final assembly on-site.

Antonio Vazquez

FCBC's Engineering Manager sets out some of the complexities involved in the construction and launch of the approach viaducts. (From Project Update Newsletter - August 2014)

Viaducts vital to bridge viability

The southern approach viaduct is rapidly taking shape on the south shore of the Forth Estuary.We find out why the viaducts are so important to the Queensferry Crossing Project and what technical challenges the team faces in their construction and installation.

Q What is the function of the viaducts?

A The viaducts will carry all north and southbound traffic to and from the bridge. They are part of the new cable-stayed main crossing, connecting the new bridge to the land on either side. They are a perfect fit with the construction method chosen. Incremental launches, such as we are carrying out at the moment, are suited for bridging shallow waters such as those found on either side of the Forth Estuary where land and water access is restricted. The main bridge itself, with its long spans, massive foundations and huge towers, performs the function of crossing the deeper water in mid estuary while leaving navigational channels open.

Q How are the viaducts constructed?

A The steel viaducts come in short sections fabricated off-site. They are pre-painted with a zinc primer, two coats of epoxy undercoat and a grey polyurethane final coat. Once on-site, the sections are welded and bolted together into longer sections up to 90m in length before final preparation for launch out over the V-shaped support piers.

Q How are the viaducts launched out?

A Powerful hydraulic machines, called strand jacks, are fixed to the bridge abutment and connected to the sections via steel cables. This jack and cable system then slowly pulls the sections out towards and over each support pier. A further strand jack and cable system attached to vertical "king posts" lifts the leading edges of the structures to counteract the effect of gravity, ensuring the viaducts are at the correct height to slide over the top of each pier. We believe this is the first time king posts have been used in this way in the UK. As each incremental launch phase is completed, we free up space on land to start the assembly of the next phase.

Q What is the biggest challenge in constructing the viaducts?

A There are lots of challenges! The first is getting the initial design right so the structures can cope with the enormous loads generated during the launch phases. This takes close co-operation between our expert teams of temporary works engineers and the designers. Secondly, we are working in a restricted space so each new section of viaduct has to arrive just at the right time to allow us to fix it to the end of the growing structure. This means we have to complete each launch out over the water on time. Thirdly, it is critically important to make sure the viaducts maintain exactly the right line of travel as they are launched out. Lateral guides and temporary bearings, coated with Teflon, are fixed on top of each pier and these ensure tracking accuracy. Only once the steel box girders for the viaducts are in place is the reinforced concrete road deck poured. Otherwise, the sections would simply be too heavy to launch without increasing the amount of structural steel. At times, it is like trying to complete a giant jigsaw puzzle which is constantly on the move! Success comes down to careful planning and the technical expertise of the whole viaducts team.

Q What stage are the viaducts at?

A   Our focus so far has been on the southern approach viaduct. At 543m in length when complete, this will be much longer than its northern neighbour (222m) which will be launched next year. To date, we have launched out 290m, so we are well over half way through the process. With a total weight of 7,000 tonnes, placing the viaduct is a demanding task and an impressive feat of engineering in its own right.

Above: **March 2014, the steel tubs for the Approach Viaduct South's north and southbound carriageways are joined together on land before being incrementally launched out over the support piers towards the South Tower.**

Launch

If the construction of the AVN differed from its southern counterpart, so did the method of delivery to its final position. If anything, the AVN launch was more complex than AVS in that it involved not only a single, rather than an incremental, launch but also a rotation – or pivot – which

Above: **February 2016, during its launch the Approach Viaduct North structure was slid down sloping ramp walls to raise the leading edge over support Pier N1.**

saw the leading edge of the entire structure raised by 2m. The complex nature of the launch process and the exposed location of the viaduct led to closely monitored wind restrictions being necessary during the operation: for the FCBC team to get the launch underway, Met Office forecasts had to predict average wind speeds of no more than 12m per second with gusts of no more than 18m per second. Contingency plans (happily not needed) were put in place to halt the launch and safely "park" and secure the structure in the event of a storm getting up during the one month long operation.

Before the launch got underway in February 2016, 40m of reinforced concrete deck was cast on top of the twin box girders at the "back" of the structure to provide vital ballast. This increased the launch weight of the structure to 6,300 tonnes. Using twin 600 tonne capacity hydraulic strand jacks attached to the tail end of the structure and strands attached to the north abutment, the structure was pulled out over a series of temporary bearings, at a speed of up to 6m per hour, until it had reached just beyond the first of its two supporting piers, N2. Inner and outer lateral guides positioned next to the bearings and on top of the two piers kept the structure on the correct alignment throughout the process. A king post

Top left and right: The Approach Viaduct North, now weighing over 6,000 tonnes, is launched out over its two reinforced concrete support piers. Note the 'king post' and attached cables keeping the leading edge raised.

Above and left: 7,000 tonnes of steel over half a kilometre in length, the Approach Viaduct South structure was launched out in stages over its eight support piers.

133

Above: **Separate steel tubs form the Approach Viaduct South's north and southbound carriageways.**

and cable system similar to that used in the AVS launch was deployed to prevent the leading edge deflecting downwards due to gravity.

Had the launch continued without rotation, the structure would eventually have struck Pier N1 about 2m below its top surface. Therefore, an innovative scheme was designed by which the trailing edge was attached to skid shoes which, as the structure continued its steady journey, travelled down two temporary ramp walls, each with an incline of 8 degrees, sited at the north abutment. As the launch continued, the structure's rear end was forced downwards. Using Pier N2 as a fulcrum in time-honoured see-saw fashion, the structure's leading edge, 222m away over the estuary, was pivoted 2m upwards to position it at the correct angle to clear the top of Pier N1 and to eventually line up with the ever lengthening balanced cantilever road deck coming northwards from the North Tower. The viaduct passed over the Pier N1 with a 20mm clearance and stopped 16m beyond having reached its final position after a dramatic 230m long journey.

From the first delivery of its steel sections to its completion, construction work on the AVN took 15 months. Believed to have been the one of the most technically challenging operation of its type ever carried out, the four week long launch was successfully completed.

Final preparation and closure

With the AVN in its final position, the laying of the reinforced concrete deck across the box girders, and the 5m hard shoulder cantilevers on either side to give the structure the required 39.8m width, could get underway. Meanwhile, the gap between the AVN and the North Tower span was ever narrowing as successive deck sections were lifted into position. In July 2016, with the lifting of the final deck section on the north side of the North Tower span, the first closure on the Queensferry Crossing was achieved connecting the AVN with the North Tower road deck.

CHAPTER 6
The Network Connections

I T is understandable – indeed, probably inevitable – that, on a bridge construction project of the scale of the Queensferry Crossing, the focus of public attention should fall primarily on the design and build of the various structures that come together to create the bridge itself. After all, it is the bridge which is the most eye-catching element and the centre piece of the entire Project. It can't help but grab the limelight and dominate the headlines.

However, any road bridge, and especially one destined to carry tens of thousands of vehicles every day for decades to come, can only succeed in carrying out the job it was designed to do if it is built in conjunction with a new, modern road system capable of providing excellent connectivity to the existing trunk and regional road network. Without the necessary roads infrastructure with the capacity to allow the smooth and efficient flow of traffic to and from the bridge, the viability of the whole Project would be called in to question. This was clearly demonstrated over fifty years ago when major new dual carriageways were built either side of the Forth Road Bridge to replace the small local roads, by then struggling to cope with the dramatic rise in car ownership and consequent

traffic levels, which led to the ferry piers in North and South Queensferry.

Major works, north and south of the Forth, were required to provide the Queensferry Crossing with the road network connections it deserves. To put it in some perspective, the connecting roads and associated works, including the installation of an Intelligent Transport System (ITS) to efficiently manage traffic, had a construction value of over £150 million, about 9% of the total Forth Replacement Crossing Project. By any measure, such a figure represents a major roads construction project. So, it is clear that the effort required to connect the Queensferry Crossing to the existing road network was substantial and just as worthy of attention as any other part of the overall Project.

What was involved? Taking both north and south road works, it would be difficult to think of any other area of the country which could throw up so many complex geographical, environmental and infrastructure factors to be taken into account. In developing the new road plans for the area, including motorway standard road approaches, new junctions, revised local road connections, various

Left: Aerial view of the newly constructed South Queensferry junction and the new stretch of A90

Above: The completed A90 extension connecting the Queensferry Crossing to the Scotstoun junction on the south side and the existing trunk roads beyond.

Below: Map of north side road works showing how the Queensferry Crossing is connected to the surrounding roads network.

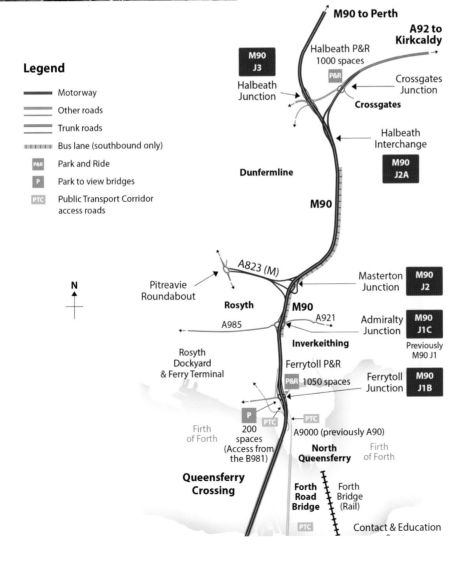

Legend

▬▬▬	Motorway
═══	Other roads
═══	Trunk roads
▪▪▪▪	Bus lane (southbound only)
P&R	Park and Ride
P	Park to view bridges
PTC	Public Transport Corridor access roads

M90 to Perth

A92 to Kirkcaldy

M90 J3

Halbeath P&R 1000 spaces

P&R

Crossgates Junction

Halbeath Junction

Crossgates

Halbeath Interchange

M90 J2A

Dunfermline

M90

A823 (M)

Masterton Junction

M90 J2

Pitreavie Roundabout

N

Rosyth

M90

A921

Admiralty Junction

M90 J1C

A985

Previously M90 J1

Inverkeithing

Rosyth Dockyard & Ferry Terminal

Ferrytoll P&R

P&R 1050 spaces

Ferrytoll Junction

M90 J1B

P PTC

A9000 (previously A90)

Firth of Forth

200 spaces (Access from the B981)

North Queensferry

Firth of Forth

Queensferry Crossing

Forth Road Bridge

Forth Bridge (Rail)

PTC

Contact & Education

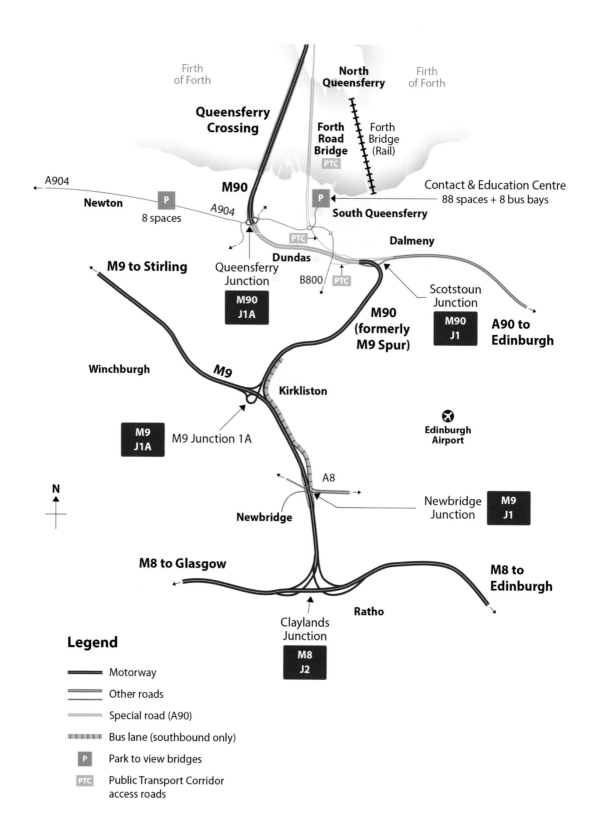

Firth of Forth

North Queensferry

Firth of Forth

Queensferry Crossing

Forth Road Bridge

PTC

Forth Bridge (Rail)

A904

Newton

P

8 spaces

M90

A904

Contact & Education Centre
88 spaces + 8 bus bays

P

South Queensferry

PTC

Dalmeny

M9 to Stirling

Queensferry Junction

Dundas

B800

PTC

M90
J1A

Scotstoun Junction

M90
(formerly
M9 Spur)

M90
J1

A90 to Edinburgh

Winchburgh

M9

Kirkliston

M9
J1A

M9 Junction 1A

Edinburgh Airport

A8

Newbridge

Newbridge Junction

M9
J1

N

M8 to Glasgow

M8 to Edinburgh

Ratho

Claylands Junction

M8
J2

Legend

———— Motorway

———— Other roads

———— Special road (A90)

▪▪▪▪▪▪ Bus lane (southbound only)

P Park to view bridges

PTC Public Transport Corridor access roads

Opposite page: Map of south side road works showing how the Queensferry Crossing is connected to the surrounding roads network.

Above: Looking east over the completed South Queensferry junction.

Left: The Ferrytoll Embankment, newly landscaped, to the north of the new bridge is one of the highest motorway embankments in the country.

bridge structures, new public transport links and improvements to the existing roads, the following on-the-ground features had to be sensitively catered for: existing local roads and their continued use throughout the construction programme, a railway line, a vast array of utility pipelines and other infrastructure and a number of ecologically important and protected areas of marshland containing nationally important wildflowers and wildlife inhabitants. Finally, and crucially, the proposals had to protect the interests of up to 50,000 local residents in the immediate vicinity and around 25,000 drivers using the Echline roundabout to the south and Ferrytoll roundabout to the north on a daily basis.

In total, the various road works covered a length of 22km and were split into three separate contracts: the installation of the Fife ITS system on the M90 north of the Forth, the upgrade of Junction 1a of the M9 on the south side and the construction of the new bridge itself and its approach roads, known as the Principal Contract.

Principal contract

Turning to the latter first, the works covered the following main features: a total of 6.4km of new or improved, motorway standard dual carriageway as well as significant lengths of new single carriageway to link with existing local roads; installation of 26 new overhead sign gantries; two new major, grade separated (two level) roundabout junctions; re-siting of a busy existing roundabout; 10 new single, double and even triple span bridges of varying sizes requiring 3,300 tonnes of structural

143

Above and right: **By April 2014, construction of the new South Queensferry junction was well underway. Here, two new single span bridges are installed which would eventually carry realigned east and westbound A904 traffic over the junction's roundabout.**

Bottom right: **The new three span B800 bridge during construction.**

Opposite page top: **Preparing to lay the reinforced concrete deck on top of the South Queensferry junction's roundabout bridges in September 2015.**

Opposite page below: **62 metres in length and weighing 160 tonnes, one of the pairs of steel beams forming the new South Queensferry junction's roundabout is lifted into place in September 2015.**

steel; several kilometres of new embankments and retaining walls; noise-reduction bunds and major service diversions and protection measures. Last, but not least, significant landscaping measures involving the planting of over 400,000 trees, shrubs and hedgerow plants.

FCBC's aim was to carry out the works while maintaining the traffic flows on the existing road network, including keeping all four lanes of the A90 dual carriageway open to traffic at all times and preserving the connectivity between local communities uncompromised. This was

Top left and right: In July 2015, with the new B800 bridge complete and opened to traffic, demolition work on the old bridge took place at night over two weekends in order to minimise disruption to traffic on the A90 below.

Above: Creating the final road surface on the new stretch of A90 south of the Queensferry Crossing was carried out by 'echelon paving' where three paving machines lay the low-noise asphalt simultaneously across the full width of the road to ensure a smooth surface with no joints.

facilitated by the fact that the new connecting roads were to be built, as much as possible, "off-line" leaving traffic to flow over existing roads largely unimpaired, though with temporary restricted speed limits introduced as a part of a package of traffic management safety measures, most notably on the existing A90.

In order to comply with the contract, FCBC also put in place measures governing the control of noise, dust and vibration which were monitored round the clock during construction activities in a move designed to protect

QUEENSFERRY PEOPLE

Claire Duguid

This article appeared in the November 2014 issue of the Queensferry Crossing Project Update newsletter.

Public focus on the Queensferry Crossing construction project often falls – understandably - on the new bridge itself. But the works to connect the bridge to the existing roads network on either side of the Forth estuary are also vital components of the whole job.

Here we speak to Claire Duguid, FCBC Senior Engineer Network Connections South.

Q First of all, tell us about your role within FCBC.

A I am based in the Network Connections South office outside South Queensferry. I help manage the various major road work schemes currently underway which are designed to allow traffic heading to and from the Queensferry Crossing, when completed, to connect easily and efficiently to the existing roads network in the area. In addition to safety on-site - our number one priority - my principal responsibilities revolve around planning: scheduling the works, managing the large number of subcontractors on-site and ordering all the materials needed to complete the works. My aim is ensure that the works remain on schedule. So far, so good!

Q What are the main elements of the road works your team is working on?

A There are several, all quite visible to local residents and passing traffic. First of all, there is the new 3km stretch of new M90 motorway and dual carriageway south of South Queensferry. This will connect the bridge to the existing M90 (formerly M9 Spur) and the A90 to Edinburgh. Then there is the major new Queensferry motorway junction to the south of the bridge which comprises slip roads, a new gyratory roundabout carrying the A904 and realigned local roads including the junction of the A904 and B924 at Echline Corner. The south carriageway of the roundabout was opened to traffic in September. The north carriageway will open later this year. Another major element of the works is the realignment of the B800 road heading towards Kirkliston which involves the construction of a new road bridge over the existing A90.

Q What are the main challenges you face?

A We have a contractual obligation to keep traffic flowing at all times on all local roads. That means we are working in a 'live traffic' situation, so effective traffic management is vital to keep any disruption to traffic to an absolute minimum. Things are easier on the new stretch of motorway we are constructing since this is being built 'off-line' away from existing roads, so there is no danger of disrupting the travelling public. Another big issue during the construction phase, especially as we approach winter, is the control of excess rainwater. We have installed a comprehensive pumping system to divert water away from the works to nearby drainage ponds on-site. Weather is always an issue, just as it is right across the Project. Being based at ground level, we are less affected by wind than our colleagues on the viaducts, towers and road decks. There are always significant logistical challenges such as managing all the personnel on-site – making sure the right people are in the right place at the right time - and that they have the right supply of materials to allow them to do their job. Finally, safety on-site is a top priority. Obligatory daily safety briefings for all personnel are helping us contribute to the excellent overall safety record the Project has to date.

Q What gives you the most satisfaction?

A Undoubtedly, it is seeing the progress being made as the new roads take shape day-by-day. The Forth Replacement Crossing is a fantastic project to be involved in and the entire roads team is proud of the part we are playing in its success to date.

Top left: **The south abutment under construction in April 2016.**

Top right: **Night-time installation of modern Intelligent Transport System (ITS) sign gantries on the M90 approach to the Queensferry Crossing minimised disruption to traffic.**

Above: **On the south side, the new stretch of A90 between the new bridge and the Scotstoun junction was the first length of new road to be completed on the Project.**

nearby residents from unnecessary inconvenience. All operations likely to generate any disturbance had to be notified several weeks in advance to a Noise Liaison Group comprising representatives of the Employer's Delivery Team (EDT), FCBC and local authorities.

The network connections operations extended over the entire duration of the Project. The creation of temporary access roads – known as haul roads - needed to get construction work underway were some of the first works completed early in the Project, while the final connecting of all newly built lengths of road to the existing roads – and, indeed, the laying of the road surface across the bridge itself - were among the last tasks to be performed prior to the Queensferry Crossing opening to traffic in the late summer of 2017. While landscaping activity ran throughout the Project, a small remaining percentage of planting work needed to be carried out after traffic started to flow through the area and this represented some of the very last works to be completed.

A notable feature during all of the road works carried out on the entire Project was the goodwill and patience displayed by commuters, local drivers and public transport operators despite long periods of speed restrictions, realigned roads and road closures and, admittedly on rare occasions, some moderate delays. There was a general interest and fascination on the part of members of the public in watching this possibly once in a lifetime construction of one of the world's great bridges. All traffic management proposals were reviewed well in advance by a Traffic Management Working Group, comprising representatives from the EDT, FCBC, local roads authorities and the emergency services. This allowed for sufficient advance notice of any potentially disruptive works which, when they did arise, were always kept to a minimum.

Network Connections – South

The Queensferry Crossing is situated immediately to the west of the ancient coastal burgh of South Queensferry which, together with the village of North Queensferry which it faces on the opposite side of the Forth, gave its name to the new bridge. The scope of the works necessary to connect the bridge to the existing trunk road network serving the area involved principally the creation of 3.4km of new dual carriageway and hard shoulder. From the south abutment of the bridge, this new stretch of A90 road initially takes traffic on a southwards course to the west of South Queensferry before swinging eastwards and continuing on the southern side of the town to meet the Scotstoun Junction where it joins both the existing A90 heading into and out of Edinburgh and the M90 Spur which joins with the M9 motorway at Junction 1a.

Above: On the north side, the new, almost completed Ferrytoll roundabout was successfully moved 100 metres north from the existing roundabout while keeping traffic flowing at all times.

Left: Looking north along the M90, construction work underway on the new Ferrytoll junction, one of the busiest junctions in Scotland.

New Queensferry Junction

Just west of Echline Corner on the western edge of the town, the plans called for the simultaneous construction of a new, two level junction to give traffic access to the motorway and the A904 and the A904/B924 Junction accessing South Queensferry from the west. This "Queensferry Junction" was to feature a large roundabout - with traffic lights and, therefore, technically known as a gyratory - situated above the newly built motorway with

four connecting slip roads. In road design terms, this is known as a grade-separated junction.

Early preparatory works got underway in 2011 with the laying of temporary access roads and traffic management measures to allow construction traffic to access the site. By the end of 2012, the line of the new road and the position of the new junction were established on the ground. The design called for the new M90 to run below the level of the gyratory in a 9m deep cutting. The plans were the subject of much discussion with the local community and extensive landscaped bunding was installed to help mitigate the intrusive effects residents might otherwise have encountered. Between the new junction and the south abutment of the Queensferry Crossing, earth bunds and noise barriers were installed to mitigate the noise of

Above: By mid 2016, the new South Queensferry junction south of the new bridge was virtually complete. A904 traffic had started flowing over the roundabout as early as autumn 2014.

traffic using the motorway.

The construction of the Queensferry Junction was a major operation involving the excavation and removal of over 200,000 cubic metres of topsoil, clay and rock. This material was re-used elsewhere across the site, including in the creation of noise-reducing bunds such as the ones built outside South Queensferry.

Once excavations were substantially complete and the four reinforced concrete abutments were in place, the new junction's bridges had to be constructed. Twelve beams up to 62m in length were delivered in short sections before final fabrication was carried out on-site ready for installation in braced pairs. Each pair cumulatively weighed 160 tonnes and, using one of the largest mobile cranes in the country, was lifted on to the abutments to create two parallel bridges that would form the east bound and west bound sections of the new gyratory. By the autumn of 2014, the road surface had been laid over these bridges and the junction was opened to take east/west traffic using the

realigned A904, although at this stage not yet fully functioning as a roundabout. Full opening of the roundabout did not occur until spring 2015, with the junction becoming fully operational only with the opening of the slip roads and the switching on of the traffic lights in 2017 once the Queensferry Crossing had been opened to traffic. At the same time, 100m to the east, the new A904/B924 junction at Echline Corner was made ready for opening in early 2015.

Interestingly, the only significant archaeological discovery made during the construction phase was in a field immediately to the north of the new junction when the remains of what was believed by experts from Historic Scotland to be one of Scotland's oldest dwellings were discovered during routine excavations. Dating from the Mesolithic period around 10,000 years ago, the house measured 7m in length and evidence of wooden support posts and fire hearths were also uncovered.

New B800 replacement bridge

At the other end of South Queensferry on the B800 (formerly the A8000) near the entrance to Dundas Castle, a new three span bridge was required over the A90 dual carriageway to replace the existing structure whose spans would not be wide enough to accommodate the proposed three lanes with hard shoulder and the single lane public transport link of the new A90 being built as part of the Project. The new composite steel beam and concrete deck bridge required six 110m long steel beams, with a total weight of 525 tonnes, to be lifted into position. Due to its location directly above existing busy roads, the operation to install the beams took place at night over the course of eight days in late 2014 in order to minimise inconvenience to the travelling public. This work was further complicated

by the need to take into account protection measures for a major utility pipeline. On completion and opening of the new B800 bridge in July 2015, the existing bridge was demolished, again at night, over two weekends. Careful traffic management planning and advance public advertising helped keep any disruption to a minimum. The resulting broken concrete was subsequently crushed and recycled for use elsewhere on the site.

The way was now clear to begin works on the complex reconfiguration of the road layout to allow for temporary diversions of north and southbound A90 traffic on to new carriageways and, ultimately, the permanent tie-in with the new motorway standard dual carriageway leading to the Queensferry Crossing.

Towards the end of 2015, construction work on the new dual carriageway had reached the stage where the road surface could begin to be laid. This was done using Transport Scotland's innovative TS2010 thin surface top layer which was laid in an operation known as "echelon paving". This involved three road paving machines laying the final surface simultaneously, thereby eliminating any longitudinal joints on the top surface, a technique which improves the performance of the surface and helps maintain the condition of the road structure through its lifespan.

Top: The new Ferrytoll viaduct abutment with some of the reinforced concrete columns on which the eighteen 100 metre long steel beams rest.

Above left: One of the steel beams being swung into place to form the Ferrytoll viaduct in September 2015.

Above: From the air, the red waterproofing membrane on the Ferrytoll viaduct is obvious.

The new and adapted stretches of road on the south side feature three overhead Intelligent Transport System (ITS) sign gantries which were installed in night-time operations lasting six nights.

South abutment

The south abutment is a reinforced concrete structure founded on a combination of intact rock and mass concrete fill. The building contains the bearing pedestals which support the southern approach viaduct's twin box girders, various rooms to house the required mechanical and electrical facilities to operate the bridge and a range of office, welfare and storage spaces. The structure also provides a pedestrian escape route from the carriageway in case of an emergency evacuation becoming necessary. The abutment was built by FCBC's Network Connections

Opposite top: Aerial view of the Ferrytoll area taken in December 2016 showing the on-going junction and viaduct works in the background, the famous St Margaret's Marsh, a Site of Special Scientific Interest (SSSI), in the foreground and, bottom left, the main Queensferry Crossing Project Office.

Opposite below: August 2017 and the first day of traffic flowing across the new Ferrytoll viaduct.

Left: Installing windshielding panels on the west side of the exposed Ferrytoll viaduct to protect passing vehicles from the effects of wind.

Below: Landscaping and road realignment in the area of the Ferrytoll Park and Ride facility.

Top: Rig installing vertical band drains to stabilise the ground beneath the road.

Above: Retaining wall at the M90 northbound slip road from Ferrytoll junction built from precast concrete panels.

team in parallel with the sequential launch of the viaduct above, being finally completed – except for internal fit-out – following the final viaduct launch in 2015.

Network Connections – North

On the north side of the Forth, the nature of the road works facing FCBC's Networks Connections team was very different to the south side where much of the works were carried out in low lying, green field conditions. In contrast, on the north shore the motorway over the Queensferry Crossing makes landfall in an area close to and constricted by the existing A90 coming from the Forth Road Bridge and the busy Ferrytoll junction. Also in this narrow area were

Above: **Traffic management formed a vital part of keeping traffic disruption to a minimum during construction work. Here, traffic flows freely along the A90 north of the Queensferry Crossing in April 2017.**

the B981 North Queensferry road, a railway line, a Park & Ride facility, a sewage treatment works, several important utilities pipelines and a number of hills, hollows and cuttings as well as an ecologically important salt marsh, all of which had to be negotiated. This presented the team with a range of challenges to be overcome in a tight space and necessitated a wholly different set of logistical construction solutions.

The scope of works included three particular challenges, all in the Ferrytoll area just north of the new bridge: the construction of a new, two-level M90 Junction, the construction of a new motorway embankment, destined to become one of the highest in Scotland, and the construction of a new two-span motorway viaduct.

In addition, new slip roads, public transport links, realigned roads, utilities infrastructure, retaining walls and the tie-in with the existing A90 would all play significant roles in the successful completion of the Network Connections North operations.

Ferrytoll Junction

Ferrytoll has always been one of the busiest and most complex junctions on the A90. Roads from Rosyth town and dockyard, North Queensferry and Inverkeithing converge on the junction, roads which during peak periods are further congested with traffic from Dunfermline and further afield seeking the shortest route to and from the Forth Road Bridge. Direct connectivity to and from the A90 dual carriageway in both directions adds to the complexity. Listeners to BBC Radio Scotland's regular morning traffic

reports will know all too well how heavily congested this area can become at peak hours.

Given that the new route of the M90 heading to and from the Queensferry Crossing would pass over the roundabout, one of the major challenges facing the Network Connections North team was how to keep the junction open at all times while carrying out the works to all the connecting roads. Part of the answer came from the decision to re-position the junction's existing roundabout 100m to the north, with the result that the northern section of the existing roundabout would, in time, become the southern leg of the new roundabout. This would also allow construction of the new roundabout, and the realignment of roads approaching it, to take place, for the most part, off-line and away from traffic flows.

Works got underway in 2014 and involved the construction of two abutments, founded on bedrock, to support two single span overbridges which would eventually carry two lanes of motorway plus hard shoulders in each direction on the new stretch of M90. By the autumn of 2015, these bridges had been completed and northbound A90 traffic was able to be diverted over them, running on narrow lanes. In early 2016, traffic using the junction below was diverted from the old roundabout on to the new one, although still under temporary traffic management and speed restrictions while other parts of

the work were progressed. Final completion of the junction could not take place until the completion of all the works on the new main M90 overhead towards the end of the Project in 2017.

As part of a wider community liaison programme covering the whole works, an on-line facility on the Project's website was established for the duration of the new junction's construction works enabling members of the public and local commuters to receive e-mail updates on the work and details of the various phases of traffic management measures necessary. These measures were subject to one unscheduled test when a quantity of live explosive charges was discovered on the site which had been left over from blasting work during the construction of the Forth Road Bridge's approach roads half a century earlier. With road closures inevitable, emergency traffic management measures were set up until the bomb squad had carried out controlled explosions and removed the danger.

Ferrytoll Embankment and viaduct

An important element in FCBC's tender for the Queensferry Crossing Project was the joint venture's proposal to substitute the client's planned multiple span viaduct at Ferrytoll to carry motorway traffic to and from the new bridge for a more cost-effective solution featuring

a smaller, 100m twin span structure along with an enormous, 200m long, 160m wide, 25m high embankment to its south.

The Ferrytoll embankment was constructed using a combination of re-cycled rock and boulder clay, sourced from the Whinnyhill cutting on the course of the new M90 immediately to the north, and spent oil shale imported from the Winchburgh bing three miles away. In all, approximately 500,000 cubic metres of fill material was used to build this giant, involving a staggering total of 50,000 lorry loads. About 25% of this total came from a nearby dolerite hill which could have been left alone but which FCBC opted to remove for its potential to provide much needed fill material, thus saving many transport miles.

Varied and generally poor ground conditions on the site of the embankment made a variety of ground improvement and strengthening measures necessary before the embankment could begin to be built. The route crossed a complex mix of land ranging from hard and rocky to soft and marshy as well as reclaimed flood plain. Conventional "dig and fill" was the solution in some parts but much more complex techniques had to be used elsewhere including the insertion of a grid of several thousand 360mm "controlled modulus columns" (CMCs). These are concrete columns inserted to a depth of up to 14m into the soft

Above: **July 2017, the Queensferry Crossing at night from the Port Edgar Marina.**

ground over which a tensioned geotextile membrane and a thin layer of fill are laid which transfer the load from the embankment down the columns to hard ground. The columns essentially bypass the soft ground, leaving it entirely undisturbed. The geotechnical work in this area used every type of technique known to the industry and was the basis of a series of award-winning technical papers on the challenges which were successfully overcome.

Construction work on the embankment was completed by the autumn of 2014 and its top surface subsequently provided a wide, flat space ideal for the construction of the northern approach viaduct during the following year.

The 100m long Ferrytoll Viaduct is situated at the northern end of the embankment and carries all motorway traffic above the realigned B981 road to North Queensferry. If the Queensferry Crossing, during its construction, was the largest bridge engineering project underway at the time in Scotland, then the Ferrytoll Viaduct was the second largest. Work began in the autumn of 2014 with the erection of 35 reinforced concrete columns on which the

viaduct would rest. The viaduct itself was constructed from 18 steel beams, weighing a total of almost 2,000 tonnes, lifted into place by crane, an operation which took several weeks longer than anticipated to complete due to the regular occurrence of very high winds. The works required the temporary diversion of the B981 back on to the old road.

Once bolted and welded together, the beams were fitted out with temporary soffits and a double mesh network of steel reinforcement bars on top of which a reinforced concrete deck was formed on which the final road surface would later be laid. This technique was essentially the same as used for the laying of the reinforced concrete surface on top of the deck sections out on the Queensferry Crossing itself.

Also similar were the finishing works carried out on the viaduct upon its completion. These included the application of a waterproofing membrane and two layers of asphalt before the final layer of "black-top" was put down. Due to the embankment's exposed position, windshielding panels were installed along the length of the viaduct's western side to protect traffic from the effects of the

prevailing winds. Protection from easterly winds is provided by the local landform.

With a surface area of 6,000 square metres, the viaduct is approximately the same size as the football pitch at Glasgow's Hampden Park. Expansion joints were installed at both ends, the one at the north end, at 112m in length, believed to be the longest expansion joint ever deployed in the UK.

B981 and new King Malcolm Drive Junction

One of the biggest changes to the roads layout on the north side made necessary by the construction of the Queensferry Crossing was the realignment of the B981 to and from North Queensferry. Whereas formerly the road had run parallel and adjacent to the A90 straight to the Ferrytoll roundabout, the route of the new stretch of M90 and its supporting embankment made that impossible. The solution was to build a new length of road taking the B981 a little to the west to meet King Malcolm Drive from where a right turn would take drivers to the new Ferrytoll Junction constructed as part of the works. This necessitated the widening of King Malcolm Drive as it approached the new

roundabout and the reconfiguring of the existing junction with Ferrytoll Road.

The realigned B981 opened to traffic in autumn 2014.

Emergency Links

In a revision to the Specimen Design, FCBC proposed the construction of two permanent emergency road links which, in the event of a future major incident resulting in the closure of the Queensferry Crossing, would provide a means to divert north and southbound traffic to the Forth Road Bridge. The completion of these links in the autumn of 2016 enabled the construction team to divert traffic passing through the site away from the difficult to access A90/new M90 tie-in area, the construction of which could be brought forward and conducted at a safe distance from passing vehicles.

Fife Intelligent Transport System (ITS)

Destined to become the first element of the overall Forth Replacement Crossing Project to be completed and fully functional, the creation of a Managed Corridor using the latest Intelligent Transport System (ITS) technology on a

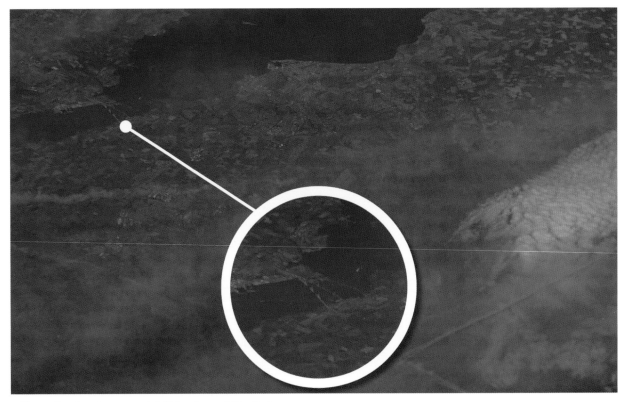

Above: The view from space! British astronaut, Tim Peake, took this photograph from the International Space Station in April 2016 in response to a request from FCBC. (Photo courtesy of NASA)

7km stretch of the M90 north of the Queensferry Crossing saw the introduction - for the first time in Scotland - of a number of modern traffic management techniques aimed at improving the supply of information to drivers approaching and crossing the Forth. This information led, in turn, to improved traffic flow, increased safety and more reliable journey times.

The £13 million contract to design and construct the Fife ITS technology and related construction works was won by John Graham (Dromore) Ltd and became fully operational in December 2012.

In all, the Managed Corridor extends a total of 22km from Junction 3 of the M90 at Halbeath over the Queensferry Crossing and all the way to Junction 1 of the M9 at Newbridge. The scheme delivered a number of Scottish trunk road "firsts" including the use of variable mandatory speed limits (VMSL), variable message signing on overhead gantries, incident detection and management measures, the use of Transport Scotland's noise reducing TS2010 road surfacing and, to help promote and encourage the use of public transport, an actively managed bus lane using the southbound hard shoulder.

Central to the effectiveness of the new system is the supply of relevant, real time information to drivers. This information is displayed on sign gantries above the carriageways which also house much of the technology behind the system including a fibre-optic communications network which connects the gantries to the new Traffic Scotland National Control Centre in South Queensferry. A total of 18 gantries were installed: seven full-span gantries over both north and southbound carriageways; ten half-span gantries over one or other carriageway; and one flag-style gantry to complement the two existing such gantries within the scheme. They ranged in length from 15m to 57m and were fixed in position on reinforced concrete bases. The majority of the works were carried out on the hard shoulder adjacent to two lanes of traffic reduced to 40mph for the safety of both the workforce and the travelling public.

Gantries were delivered to the contractor's yard pre-assembled and ready to be fitted out with secondary steelwork and the ITS equipment. This was fully tested before the gantries were transported by lorry to their location for erection. In order to minimise traffic disruption on the M90, gantry erection was carried out at night using either full carriageway closure or rolling road blocks.

At three gantry locations, mine consolidation works were required to stabilise previously worked mine seams in order to remove the risk of subsidence. In addition, landscaping measures were undertaken at each gantry site ranging from grass seeding to tree and shrub planting depending on the specific location and surrounding

ITS WORKING WELL

This article first appeared in the Queensferry Crossing's Project Update Newsletter of March 2013.

The Scottish winter has thrown us all its usual challenges but this hasn't stopped the Forth Replacement Crossing from delivering some key elements of the Project ahead of schedule.

On 4th December last year, the Fife ITS contract on the M90 reached completion. As well as significantly upgrading the road itself, the scheme introduces new features for Scotland's trunk road network with the introduction of variable mandatory speed limits and bus priority lanes, delivered as part of the phased introduction of ITS (Intelligent Transport Systems) across the FRC corridor from Halbeath on the M90 in the north to Junction 1a of the M9 on the south side.

ITS uses overhead gantry-mounted equipment to assist in the management of traffic. The state-of-the-art technology detects traffic building up and then lowers the mandatory speed limit to smooth flow and reduce queuing. The gantries also control bus lane operation, ensuring the hard shoulder is always available in emergencies.

The system is managed by staff at the Traffic Scotland Control Centre where traffic flows, ITS data and displays are continually monitored. The system will be evaluated to ensure positive adjustments can be made to improve it further.

The full benefits of ITS won't be felt until the new bridge is complete but Transport Scotland's FRC Roads Infrastructure Manager, Steven Brown, said the system is already working well. Steven said: "For the past 16 months, regular commuters on the M9 and M90 in the vicinity of the Forth Road Bridge have patiently witnessed the construction of the M9 Junction 1a and Fife ITS projects. It's still early days in this initial 'optimising' phase, however initial benefits are already being seen as traffic speeds at peak-time are being reduced on the approach to queues, helping to alleviate congestion and reduce the risk of accidents. More information is being provided to motorists via the electronic signs and public transport users are benefiting from quicker journeys as buses are utilising the bus lanes to bypass slow moving traffic."

Monitoring work will continue to ensure this level of service on this vital stretch of road is maintained.

features. Between the Admiralty and Masterton junctions, a noise barrier was erected adjacent to the northbound carriageway to reduce the noise impact from traffic on nearby properties.

Matching evidence from other ITS schemes in the UK and abroad, surveys demonstrated immediate proof of the beneficial impact of the Fife ITS scheme from the moment it became operational in December 2012 with reduced congestion, greater safety and improved traffic flow for drivers and public transport users alike. Upon completion of the Queensferry Crossing, these benefits were extended across the Firth of Forth to the realigned A90 heading into and out of Edinburgh and the renamed M90 Spur leading to Junction 1a of the M9.

M9 Junction 1a

The upgrade of the existing Junction 1a on the M9, some 6km south of the new bridge, formed an essential part of the overall Forth Replacement Crossing Project. By providing new west facing slip roads, it significantly increased capacity and improved connectivity for M9 traffic heading to and from the new bridge and benefitted from the introduction of a further section of the Intelligent Transport Systems described above.

The £25.6 million contract to construct the improved junction was won after a successful tender by SRB, a joint venture between John Sisk & Son and Roadbridge and was successfully completed in February 2013.

The improvements to the junction removed a notorious bottleneck for traffic. The principal elements of the complex works included the following:

- the widening of the M9 between Junction 1 (Newbridge) and Junction 1a with the carriageway widened to four lanes and a hard shoulder in each direction to assist traffic flow and improve lane change opportunities between the junctions

- construction of new link roads with hard shoulders between the existing M90 Spur and M9 to provide, for the first time, a direct link for traffic wishing to access the bridge from the west or heading west from the bridge. These new link roads have helped reduce the previous traffic flows at the Newbridge roundabout and also reduced the number of heavy goods vehicles using the A904 through Newton village by nearly two-thirds

- the construction of an additional bridge over the M9 at Junction 1a for Queensferry Crossing bound traffic and the reconfiguration of the existing bridge to accommodate the new westbound traffic

- 2km of new, dedicated southbound bus lane to enhance public transport flow between the junction and Newbridge especially during periods of heavy traffic

- widening of the existing B9080 and Overton Road underbridges adjacent to Kirkliston in order to accommodate the new northbound carriageway of the M9

Above and right: Before and after, Junction 1a of the M9 motorway south of the new bridge was reconfigured as part of the Forth Replacement Crossing Project to increase capacity and improve connectivity between the new bridge and surrounding motorways. New slip roads were provided to the M9 for traffic to and from Stirling and Falkirk.

Above: The scale of the Queensferry Crossing compared to the Forth Road Bridge is obvious from this photo taken on a relatively rare day of low wind.

Spur and connecting roads

• installation of 17 gantries with associated Intelligent Transport System infrastructure

The Project was subject to stringent environmental requirements with the creation or construction of steel culverts in the area of the Swine Burn, the burn itself being realigned and deepened to improve fresh water fish habitats and its banks sown with wildflowers. In addition, three sustainable urban drainage system (SUDS) basins were constructed to allow surface water settlement before discharging into local watercourses. Mammal tunnels were installed to help protect the movements of the local badger and otter populations, while a new otter holt was installed to replace an existing holt unavoidably disturbed by the construction works. Finally, extensive landscape planting, involving some 70,000 trees, shrubs and hedgerow plants, was undertaken which, together with the careful placement

of noise barriers and bunds, reduced the impacts on the surrounding community and successfully integrated the new sections of road into the landscape.

Throughout the works, traffic management played a vital role in maintaining the free-flowing movement of approximately 30,000 vehicles per day using the Junction. The new M9 overbridge was constructed in stages, the work being carried out to coincide with periods of reduced traffic volumes, such as during the night when rolling roadblocks became necessary for the installation of the pre-fabricated bridge beams.

Most passing motorists may not even have realised that the improvements to this busy motorway junction formed part of the construction of the Queensferry Crossing. Nevertheless, without them, traffic access to and from the new bridge would be significantly the poorer and the improvements to a number of local minor roads would not have occurred.

M90 Junction 1a complete

This article appeared in the Queensferry Crossing's Project Update of March 2013.

A major milestone in the FRC Project has been achieved with the completion of the M9 Junction 1a upgrade works. SRB Civil Engineering completed the works ahead of schedule which meant that the junction became fully operational on the 1st February when it was officially opened by Scottish Transport Minister, Keith Brown MSP.

The works to improve this vital link to and from the new Forth Crossing began in July 2011. Since then, the landscape of the area around the junction has seen some significant changes, including:

• major earthworks to construct the new west facing link roads
• construction of a new bridge structure over the M9
• installation of 17 gantries which form the backbone for the new ITS system which is being installed throughout the complete Forth Replacement Crossing scheme from Halbeath in Fife to Junction 1a of the M9
• modifications to existing structures and culverts.

In excess of 400,000 man hours were put into this difficult project which was carried out with live traffic running through the site on a daily basis.

Traffic management was one of the major challenges for the team; whilst some queuing was inevitable in a project of this scale and complexity, in general commuting traffic experienced minimal disruption. Since the junction has been opened fully, there has been a significant drop in the levels of traffic queuing in peak hours in the village of Kirkliston and on the M9 Spur southbound.

SRB would like to thank everyone involved in the project, the Employer's Delivery Team, designers, subcontractors and the local communities to mention just a few. Everyone in SRB Civil Engineering Ltd is proud to have played a part in this project and we wish all the best to everyone involved in the rest of the Forth Replacement Crossing Project in the years ahead.

Below: The EDT and M9 Junction 1a teams celebrate the completion and opening of the reconfigured junction.

CHAPTER 7

Working in the Community

ENGAGING with local communities and a whole host of interested national and international organisations lay at the very heart of the construction of the Queensferry Crossing. The pride and excitement felt by everyone involved in the construction works were reflected in the determination to involve and educate as many people of all ages as possible. In setting the scene for the placing of the four separate contracts which comprise the overall Forth Replacement Crossing Project (Principal Contract, ie. the new bridge itself and its connecting roads, Fife ITS, M9 Junction 1a and the Contact & Education Centre), the Employer's Delivery Team (EDT) created a Code of Construction Practice and a suite of Employer's Requirements, the successful delivery of which would ensure that the various contractors' performances would be maintained at the highest level.

As it transpired, the contractors not only sought to match the stringent requirements but actually exceeded them on many fronts.

Community Engagement and the Contact & Education Centre

For the first eighteen months of the Project, community activity was based at the offices of the Forth Estuary Transport Authority (FETA), immediately to the south of the

Forth Road Bridge providing a drop-in point for members of the public and a hub for community engagement activities. In the early days, Project staff carried out frequent school visits to raise awareness amongst pupils of the feats of civil engineering getting underway out on the Forth.

In January 2013, the brand new, purpose-built Contact & Education Centre (CEC), built by Dawn Construction Ltd and adjacent to the FETA building, was opened to the public. Designed as the focal point for community engagement and education activity for the rest of the Project's life and beyond, the aim of the CEC was "to provide high quality contact and education services to local residents and visitors while emphasising the Project's purpose, investment value and innovation in construction, as well as the potential benefits which a career in engineering can provide."

Such a challenging and high profile construction project as the Queensferry Crossing was always bound to attract national and international interest; the CEC provided an ideal, tailor-made facility for welcoming visitors and setting out the scope of the Project.

For the rest of the construction programme, the CEC hosted the Forth Replacement Crossing Exhibition which sought to share the construction techniques being

Opposite page: Local schoolchildren proudly display their winning entries in FCBC's schools painting competition in 2013.

Left: The Contact & Education Centre (CEC) in South Queensferry welcomed many thousands of school pupils keen to learn more about the Queensferry Crossing and civil engineering in general.

Below: The CEC not only housed a permanent exhibition but was an ideal location for presentations and talks to local groups and industry bodies.

Public and stakeholder update meetings were held at key stages of the Project and a series of quarterly Community Forums brought together representatives from affected communities, the EDT and the contractors as a means of sharing information about the Project's progress and discussing relevant local issues.

A number of Working Groups were established to

employed on the Project through information panels, detailed bridge models, audio/visual materials and presentations by Project team members, as well as providing spectacular views of the existing bridges over the Forth. School pupils visited from all over Scotland to find out more about the Project and undertake Science, Technology, Engineering, Art and Mathematics (STEAM) related challenges as well as taking part in bridge building exercises.

oversee traffic, marine, noise and environmental matters. These Groups assisted in the planning and monitoring of all potentially sensitive activities to ensure that the impact of the works on the local communities and natural environment was minimised. Noise, vibration and air quality were monitored remotely by high-tech monitoring instruments set up in gardens adjacent to the works and the information gathered was made available for public scrutiny on the Project website.

Top: **Another group of excited pupils arrives at the CEC.**

Top right: **Local residents enjoy a wintry tour off-site as part of the Project's community engagement programme of events.**

Above: **The permanent Project exhibition inside the CEC proved a popular attraction for local residents and other visitors.**

As the largest infrastructure development in Scotland for a generation, the Project represented an ideal opportunity for many subcontractor and supplier businesses to get involved and provide a significant boost to the economy. Early on, a series of "Meet the Buyer" events were held where interested parties could meet members of the contractors' procurement teams and gain an appreciation of the nature, volume and timing of forthcoming commercial bidding opportunities.

Interest groups from all over the world – universities, civil engineering institutions, professional bodies and private groups - began to arrange visits to the CEC, while locally a large variety of groups, including Rotary, Probus, various societies, men's groups, women's groups and mixed groups, took advantage of what the CEC had to offer on their doorstep. By the time of the Official Opening of the Queensferry Crossing, the CEC had welcomed over 83,000 visitors through its doors, 25,000 of whom were schoolchildren.

Communications

Keeping local residents up-to-speed with anything that could impact on them was an on-going priority. At monthly communications meetings, the contractors submitted their "Three Month Forward Look" schedules to the client. Looking to the immediate period ahead, these identified forthcoming construction activities with the potential to impact local communities. From these meetings, the need for any neighbour notifications could be agreed. In many cases, such as overnight traffic switches, temporary road signage, either static or Variable Message Signs on the motorway network, sufficed but where noise disturbance was a possibility, all practicable mitigation measures would be applied along with notification via leafleting.

The public's main point of contact with the Project was the Community Liaison Team which was always on hand to provide information and support in response to enquiries, concerns or complaints received. A 24-hour Project telephone hotline and dedicated email address were set up

Above: The "Frame the Bridge" mosaic was made up from thousands of "selfie" photographs sent in by members of the public and Project staff.

Right: One of the regular Community Forum meetings gets underway.

Bottom right: Another schools "Build the Bridge" exercise successfully completed in the CEC.

and, of course, the latest Project information was always available at the CEC. In addition, noticeboards situated at various locations within the vicinity were kept updated with information while flyer notifications were regularly delivered to nearby residents and businesses in areas affected by construction work. Popular Project Update newsletters were produced on a quarterly basis, providing general and technical updates on the construction progress and reports of key achievements, along with a range of the latest photographs covering all aspects of the construction works.

The Queensferry Crossing website, a section of Transport Scotland's website, provided the history of the Project from inception to completion as well as key facts and figures and general information such as construction progress, updates for road users, forthcoming community engagement events, maps, and all published documents.

Above: **School pupils visit the main Project Office in February 2012.**

Right: **The quarterly "Project Update" newsletters proved popular with young and old alike.**

Bottom right: **Members of the construction team help former First Minister, Alex Salmond, reveal the name of the new bridge in June 2013.**

Webcams provided live, online coverage of the works and proved very popular with the public, as did the Project's dedicated You-Tube channel which contained a variety of fascinating video footage. In addition, a section on the Queensferry Crossing was included in the Forth Bridges' website. Many people used You-Tube and social media in engaging with the Project either directly or through Community Council websites.

"Name the Bridge" was an initiative which proved very popular with the public because it gave them a chance to have their say on what the new bridge should be officially called. A staggering 7,600 or more separate name ideas were received. Over 35,000 people took part in the ballot during the seven month process with "Queensferry Crossing" ultimately securing more than a third of the votes cast and coming out on top.

Another popular initiative was "Frame the Bridge"

QUEENSFERRY
CROSSING
M90

Above: **Honoured guests: veterans of the Forth Road Bridge construction project in the 1950s and '60s enjoyed site tours in 2013 and 2015.**

through which the public were invited to send in "selfie" photos of themselves which were used to form a striking photographic mosaic of the new bridge which can be seen on page 172.

Monitor Hosts

Continuous environmental monitoring played an important part in the community liaison aspect of the Project. Symbolising the close co-operation between the Project and the local community, in 2012 an initiative was set up involving local residents willing to host noise and air quality monitoring instruments in or near their gardens and provide the power source to operate them. 16 local residents kindly volunteered to assist and, as part of this initiative, each year they were each asked to nominate a good cause to receive a donation of £500 from FCBC. The hosts were invited to an annual Progress Update presentation in the CEC and given a tour of the construction-site.

Veterans' Visits

How does the construction of the Queensferry Crossing

compare with building the Forth Road Bridge back in the 1950s and '60s? That was what 35 of the Forth Road Bridge construction team veterans came to find out in May 2015 in a follow-up to their first site visit in March 2013. Queensferry Crossing staff were honoured and privileged to welcome their predecessors to the Queensferry Crossing. A presentation at the CEC provided an in-depth look at the construction of the new bridge and its connecting roads. A coach tour of the construction-site on both shores of the Forth was followed by lunch, giving the veterans a chance to share stories and experiences not only with each other, but with the current engineering staff. Whilst many things have changed in 50 years, a sense of pride in their work and the scale of their achievements provided common ground for those involved in these two exceptional construction projects.

Bridges to Schools

This educational event was held annually in association with the Institution of Civil Engineers (ICE). Around 300 pupils each year enjoyed building their own cable-stayed bridge, giving them an insight into the technical challenges of civil engineering as well as the importance of health and safety and teamwork, while having some fun along the way. Dressed in hard hats and hi-viz vests, the pupils were asked to construct a 12m long, 3.5m high model of a cable-

Above: What more appropriate location could there be for young people to learn about civil engineering?

Right: Members of the design and construction teams collecting one of the Project's Considerate Constructors Scheme Gold Awards.

Bottom right: Civil engineering students from the University of Strathclyde on a site tour in April 2014.

stayed bridge, supervised by volunteer civil engineers from the Project. The pupils (and some intrepid teachers) then walked across the completed bridge to test the strength of what they had constructed.

Awards

Everyone involved in the construction of the Queensferry Crossing was proud that the Project received five Gold Awards in a row from the Considerate Constructors Scheme between 2013 and 2017. The objective of this industry-wide scheme is to promote the highest possible standards within the construction industry and the high esteem of the public via continuous improvement.

Employment

Careers in the industry were actively encouraged with

Above: **FCBC donations in support of local charities were a valued part of the community engagement programme.**

Top right: **A large number of civil engineering graduates and apprentices were employed to work with the construction teams in the office and on-site.**

numerous university and college visits and support for students, such as student mentoring, work experience and temporary placements designed to lead to graduate employment. At periods of peak activity, approximately 1,500 people were directly employed on building the Queensferry Crossing. This does not take into account the additional people working for the hundreds of Scottish firms in the subcontracting and supply chain. Furthermore, there was a requirement under the Contract to create an annual average of 45 vocational training positions, 21 professional body training places and 46 positions for long-term unemployed people, as well as opportunities to maximise modern apprenticeship opportunities each year. These targets were exceeded each year.

Forth Bridges Operating Contract (FBOC)

The maintenance of the completed Queensferry Crossing, the Forth Road Bridge and the road network from Halbeath on the M90 to Junction 1a of the M9, a total of 22km, will be the responsibility of the Forth Bridge Operating Contractor which will be the future first point of contact for members of the community. The FBOC Contractor is based in the former offices of Forth Estuary Transport Authority adjacent to the CEC. Under the terms of the Queensferry Crossing contract, FCBC have a five-year obligation to carry out any defect repairs and certain items of maintenance.

Stemming from the enthusiasm and excitement felt by everybody directly involved in the construction of the Queensferry Crossing, liaison with people – whether local residents, students and schoolchildren from all over the country, professional bodies or social groups – was always a top priority throughout the life-span of the Project.

CHAPTER 8

Working in
the Environment

THERE was a time, happily long since past, when environmental considerations came well down the list of priorities in construction projects. Today, however, care for the environment is one of the most important issues facing any construction contract which is, of course, as it should be. On a project of the scale and significance of the Queensferry Crossing, protecting – even enhancing - the local environment is an imperative.

From the outset, Transport Scotland's Forth Replacement Crossing Environmental Statement and Code of Construction Practice (CoCP) set out how the new bridge was to be delivered in an environmentally sensitive way and contained some of the most rigorous and comprehensive environmental care provisions ever seen in the UK. FCBC set out not only to meet these challenging contractual requirements but, where possible, to exceed them and to deliver the new bridge and its surrounding roads to the highest possible environmental standards.

FCBC's ambition was that the processes and systems adopted in the design and construction of the Queensferry Crossing would be considered, in years to come, the international benchmarks for environmental care and

sustainability in major infrastructure projects.

Throughout the construction works, the principal considerations fell into four categories: people, water, terrestrial ecology and marine ecology.

To assist with the tasks, two principal liaison groups (covering noise and the environment) were established, chaired by Transport Scotland and involving FCBC, local authorities, community councils, local community groups, Scottish Natural Heritage, Marine Scotland and other relevant parties depending on the function of the group. These liaison groups met at monthly intervals to monitor progress and compliance with the CoCP. Members were also encouraged to offer input with the aim of helping the Project achieve its best practice targets.

People

The objective was to minimise the impact of construction activities on the lives of local residents. A range of state of the art monitoring equipment was set up at key locations near to the main construction works. 24 hours a day, seven days a week for the duration of the works, this equipment would measure noise, vibration and

Left: Newly constructed noise barriers protect local residents from traffic noise.

Below: Care for local wildlife, both marine and land-based, was an important part of the Project. In addition to constant monitoring of their conditions in relation to construction activity, the installation of artificial badger setts, tunnels under roads and bat boxes, as well as the planting of over 400,000 trees, shrubs and hedgerow plants, ensured any environmental impacts were minimised. Even nesting ducks in the middle of FCBC's Marine Yard were protected.

air quality, sending data back to FCBC's Environmental team. Standards were set for each of these elements, as required by the CoCP and FCBC's Environmental Management Plan and, in many cases, work practices on the ground were changed to better these standards.

Examples included amending the Specimen Design to provide additional heightened noise barriers and bunds at certain locations, the use of extra noise barriers designed on the permanent works and the issuing of regular environmental bulletins to staff and environmental awards aimed at achieving continual improvement. A very close working relationship with the Scottish Environmental Protection Agency (SEPA) proved beneficial in ensuring the team's green aims were met.

The use of 'quiet 'plant, such as power generators with extra soundproofing, and rubber hammers also played a role in keeping noise levels as low as possible.

As far as air quality was concerned, all construction tasks were analysed ahead of time to minimise the creation of any dust or road mud. Wheel washes were provided at construction-site exits to clean the wheels of construction vehicles before they entered public roads.

In addition, full-time road sweepers and water sprayers were employed to reduce dust and to keep the roads as clean as possible.

Fully engaging with communities likely, on occasions, to be affected in order to make them aware of any planned construction activities, and to include their concerns in planning for these activities, was a vital part of securing the understanding of local residents (see Chapter 7 - Working in the Community – for more details of the steps taken to keep local people informed and involved).

Above: **Regular surveying by specialist ecologists helped protect the local bat population.**

Right: **Several acres of bluebells were successfully transplanted to a local woodland.**

Bottom right: **St Margaret's Marsh near North Queensferry is a Site of Special Scientific Interest (SSSI) and required special attention during the nearby construction works.**

Water

The new bridge crosses a wide estuary renowned for its varied sea and birdlife. On land, the road works to construct the approach roads on either shore had the potential to affect a number of watercourses flowing into the sea. Preserving the marine environment in the Forth and protecting the quality of all groundwater flowing into it from both sides was an absolute priority.

Weekly inspections were carried out to assess any possible run-off from the site into watercourses and to check groundwater levels at several locations via boreholes. This regular monitoring ensured that the works did not adversely alter the hydrology or hydro-geology in any particular area of the site. Water samples were laboratory tested to ensure quality was maintained.

Nearby, two Sites of Special Scientific Interest (SSSI), designated for their national importance in terms of geology, geomorphology and ecology, required protection. Regular testing of water samples drawn from boreholes ensured the sites' integrity was maintained at all times.

Sustainable Urban Drainage Systems (SUDS) were designed both for temporary use during the construction

Above: Throughout the construction programme, 400,000 trees, shrubs and hedgerow plants were planted in and around the site on both sides of the Firth of Forth.

phase but also for long term operational use once construction work was completed. These are specially created basins providing temporary storage of surface water which is released over the following 24 hours into

Landscaping

The Queensferry Crossing construction programme included the planting of 400,000 trees, shrubs and hedgerow plants. These included:

Trees

Aesculus hippocastanum - horse chestnut
Alnus glutinosa - alder
Betula pendula – birch
Fagus sylvatica - beech
Fraxinus excelsior – ash (until ban on movement of
  ash trees in 2012)
Prunus avium - wild cherry
Quercus robur - oak
Sorbus aucuparia - rowan
Taxus baccata -yew

Shrubs

Carpinus betulus - hornbeam
Corylus avellana - hazel
Crataegus monogyna - hawthorn
Hedera helix – ivy
Lonicera periclymenum - honeysuckle
Prunus spinosa - blackthorn
Rosa canina - dog rose
Viburnum opulus - guelder rose

A number of invasive species, including Japanese knotweed and giant hogweed were identified on-site. Control measures were implemented to prevent the spread of these species through the movement of construction vehicles, machinery and personnel and tight control and monitoring procedures were adopted during any topsoil stripping and relocation. An eradication programme for the species was also undertaken throughout the period of the construction works.

St Margaret's Marsh, almost in the shadow of the new bridge, is a Site of Special Scientific Interest (SSSI) located on the northern shore of the Firth of Forth at Rosyth. It comprises an area of salt marsh and reed beds situated immediately behind a sea-wall. Transport Scotland acquired the marsh and is managing it with a view to increasing the salt marsh habitat by allowing more sea water in. FCBC provided three new sea inlets by installing sluice gates to control and manage the flow of sea water which is predicted to help the situation in years to come.

In addition to the expert staff from the Project's permanent Environment Department, key to the success of the Queensferry Crossing's environmental care and sustainability programme was communication with all site personnel, subcontractors and suppliers. In order to ensure a clear understanding of the aims of the programme, regular environmental bulletins were issued to the staff carrying out the work "on the ground". Aimed at promoting the positive environmental vision of the Project and instilling a shared commitment to protecting the environment at all times, these bulletins covered topics such as waste segregation, pollution control and dust and noise prevention.

The success of the Queensferry Crossing construction programme was complemented by the success of the environmental care programme which saw many targets exceeded and potential impacts as far as possible minimised. Widely recognised as raising the standards of environmental care on major infrastructure projects to new levels, the Queensferry Crossing has left a lasting legacy for the future.

the drainage system, thus minimising the risk of flood. They also act as settling basins where suspended solids are given time to settle before clean water is discharged back into the local water systems.

Particular care was taken in the planning of construction activities on the Forth itself to ensure the integrity of the river and to prevent any pollution which might affect marine wildlife. This was particularly so during tower and deck construction where the overriding priority was to make sure no construction materials would find their way into the water.

Wildlife

The Firth of Forth contains important areas of intertidal and subtidal habitats and supports important populations of migratory and non-migratory fish, including important populations of salmon and lamprey heading up river to the Special Area of Conservation at the River Teith near Stirling. A wide range of marine mammals, estuarine birds and sediment-dwelling organisms are also present. Professional surveys carried out before construction work got underway confirmed the presence of a wide range of bird species including no fewer than 26 wildfowl species, 11 species of gull, 14 species of wader as well as cormorants, puffins, herons, swans, birds of prey, kingfishers and ravens. A number of these species are protected by legislation. Transport Scotland carried out annual estuarine bird surveys in order to inform on-going assessment of the

construction works and the finished Queensferry Crossing on these protected species.

As far as the marine ecology was concerned, the priority was to protect any species living in the sea or relying on it for food sources, such as seals, porpoises, seabirds and migrating fish, from pollution, cloudy water and noise. Terrestrial ecology focused on the range of land animals found in the area: species such as badgers, deer, otters and birds. In all cases, the objective was to minimise disturbance to these species and wherever possible – for example, with the installation of bat boxes in advance of the construction works starting - to improve their conditions.

A number of artificial badger setts were placed in strategic locations to encourage rehoming where established setts had to be removed for the construction of new roads. Indeed, the first of these was installed even before construction work had begun. The environment team was delighted when badger activity was subsequently confirmed at the new setts.

Several mammal tunnels were built beneath the newly constructed roads on the south side of the works and fences were put in place to direct the animals towards the tunnels.

Each year, aspects of the construction works were reprogrammed so as to avoid disturbance to migrating and nesting birds during the breeding season.

Early surveys confirmed the presence of two species of

bat in the area, both protected, of course. Regular monitoring throughout the life of the Project ensured no negative effect on the local population. The installation of bat boxes was an important feature of the overall package of care towards local wildlife. Underwater noise monitoring was especially important. Harbour porpoises, bottlenose and white beaked dolphins, Minke whales and a variety of seals are all frequent visitors to the estuary. During the construction of the towers' foundations when construction activity was most likely to emit noise into the sea, Passive Acoustic Monitoring equipment tracked the movement of sea life in the estuary. If mammals were detected within 1km of the site, any scheduled blasting was postponed. The first blasting operation on Beamer Rock at the start of work to build the Central Tower's foundations had to be delayed for 48 hours in order to allow a large number of seals to disperse and leave the location.

One hour before any noise-emitting activity could begin, an innovative mobile underwater sound system was employed which sent out low frequency sound waves to deter fish from approaching the area. FCBC employed a full time Ecological Clerk of Works to administer this element of the work.

Plant life

Turning to the local flora and plant life, covering all the trees, shrubs, flowers and ground flora which could potentially be impacted by construction activity, the objective was again to improve conditions rather than merely maintain the status quo.

Any trees which were felled due to construction works were replaced. Where reasonably practicable, the species of replacement trees were selected to achieve a close resemblance of the original trees using locally occurring native species.

Over eight hectares of bluebells were identified in the immediate locality north of the Queensferry Crossing, roughly 25% of them in the St Margaret's Hope area. In 2012, an area of 0.75 hectares of bluebells needed to be transplanted. Following the clearance of vegetation, the topsoil containing the bulbs was carefully stripped back and successfully relocated to the woodland at nearby Castlandhill.

On a project of this scale, landscaping represented a major part of the environmental care focus. A local plant nursery was awarded the contract to supply all the plants necessary. By the completion of the Project, a massive total of 400,000 trees, shrubs and hedgerow plant species had been planted which not only acted as an early softening of the impact of the new roads, junctions and bridges on the landscape, but has also provided a habitat for local wildlife as well as screening the road for nearby properties.

CHAPTER 9

Something Worth Celebrating

THE Queensferry Crossing was officially opened by Her Majesty Queen Elizabeth II, accompanied by HRH The Duke of Edinburgh, on Monday 4th September 2017. The significance of the date was not lost on any of the 3,600 invited guests present at the Official Opening Ceremony for it was exactly 53 years earlier, on the 4th September 1964, that the Queen had officially opened the Queensferry Crossing's neighbour, the Forth Road Bridge.

The tradition of opening Forth Bridges on the fourth of the month stretches back 127 years to the 4th March 1890 when HRH The Prince of Wales (later King Edward VII) declared the Forth Bridge officially open. Who knows, but hopefully in centuries to come any future bridges in this locality will follow suit with this Victorian witticism.

Early morning mist on the Forth, so reminiscent of the thick fog which had cloaked the Forth Road Bridge's opening ceremony half a century earlier, gave way to a steady drizzle which did nothing to dampen the excitement and enthusiasm of the crowds gathered to play their part in this little bit of history making. Arriving at the South Abutment, Her Majesty was greeted by cheering pupils from eight local schools before being welcomed by the

Lord Lieutenant of Edinburgh, Frank Ross, and the Rt Hon Nicola Sturgeon MSP, Scotland's First Minister. Following introductions to the Chiefs of the three Armed Services in Scotland and senior representatives from the Scottish Government and Transport Scotland, the Queen met David Climie, Project Director from the Employer's Delivery Team, and Michael Martin, FCBC's Project Director, whose grand-daughter, six year-old Elizabeth Rose Martin, presented a bouquet of flowers. Adding to the celebratory atmosphere, ceremonial music was magnificently played by the Band of the Royal Regiment of Scotland and the West Lothian Schools Pipe Band. Also in attendance were members of The Royal Company of Archers, the Sovereign's ceremonial bodyguard in Scotland.

Forming a short line-up, representatives of the FCBC and Design Joint Venture staff were presented to the Queen before she was invited to cut a ribbon marking both the official opening of the bridge and the cue for a spectacular low level fly-past by the RAF Red Arrows – without which no great national event in the United Kingdom is ever complete - above the bridge's towers. At the same time, on the waters below, a flotilla of 130 vessels

North and South Queensferry where many hundreds of people had gathered to catch a glimpse of the proceedings, Transport Scotland had organised tea parties for local residents with live television relay of the ceremonial events taking place on and off the new bridge.

The Royal couple drove north across the bridge to FCBC's Project Offices in Rosyth where they were met by the Lord Lieutenant of Fife, Robert Balfour, who introduced her to members of the Project team and the Provosts of Fife and West Lothian. A special concert of music, song, film and the spoken word was performed by some of Scotland's leading contemporary artistes. This included a new poem by Scots Makar, Jackie Kay, entitled simply "Queensferry Crossing" (see page 204) and a song of tribute to the bridge written and performed by local school children. The Band of Her Majesty's Royal Marines Scotland and the Boghall & Bathgate Caledonia Pipe Band played several popular pieces to the great delight of the thousands

Opposite page: A spectacular lighting show kicked off a week of memorable events marking the completion of the bridge.

Top: The Red Arrows pay tribute to the Queensferry Crossing in their own special way.

Above: Her Majesty and The Duke of Edinburgh meet members of the design and construction team.

'dressed overall' with flags from bow to stern gathered around the three famous Forth bridges as a mark of respect both for Her Majesty and the new bridge. Meanwhile, in

of people in the audience.

In her speech, the Queen hailed the Queensferry Crossing as a "remarkable achievement" and paid tribute to the many thousands of men and women involved in the design and construction of the bridge. "The three magnificent structures we see here – spanning three centuries – are all feats of modern engineering and a tribute to the talents, vision and remarkable skills of those who designed and built them. The Queensferry Crossing joins its iconic and historic neighbours to create not only a

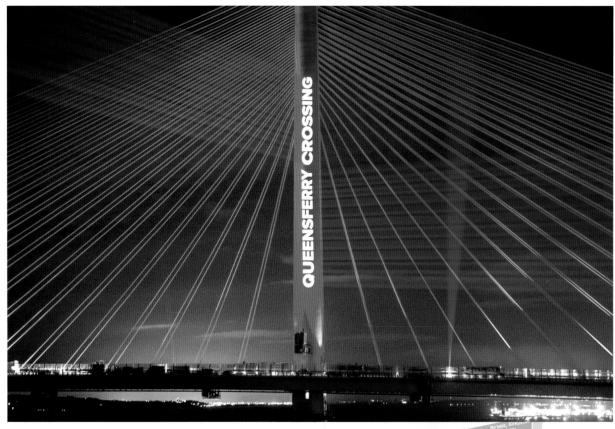

Above: The lighting show was watched by hundreds of people on both shores of the Forth.

Right: Two Elizabeths - Elizabeth Rose Martin presents a bouquet of flowers to the Queen.

breath-taking sight over the Firth of Forth, but to provide an important link for so many in this community and the surrounding areas."

In turn, the First Minister thanked the 15,000 men and women who had built the bridge saying the professionalism, dedication and expertise they had brought to the Project was "awe inspiring".

Before departing, the Queen unveiled one of six commemorative plaques which were shortly afterwards affixed to prominent positions on the Queensferry Crossing. Further representatives of the Employer's Delivery Team and FCBC were presented before, to their obvious delight, the Queen and Duke of Edinburgh were presented with a specially commissioned, solid silver model of the Queensferry Crossing by Keith Brown MSP, Cabinet Secretary for Economy, Jobs and Fair Work.

The Official Opening Ceremony represented the climax of an exciting week-long festival of events to celebrate the completion and opening of the new bridge. These had begun on 28th August with a late night light show, switched on by the First Minister surrounded by over 100

members of the Project team, which illuminated the bridge's immense structure along its entire length with hundreds of multi-coloured flood lights in a spectacular display which lasted 90 minutes.

Two days later, on 30th August, the Queensferry Crossing, after four years in the planning and six in construction, finally fulfilled the purpose for which it was designed by opening to traffic. The first vehicles to cross – at 1-30am - were escorted over the bridge's northbound carriageway by police cars. An hour later the southbound carriageway opened in similar fashion leading to the first rush hour a few hours later when all those tens of

Above: **50,000 people walked across the bridge during the 'Queensferry Crossing Experience' weekend of 2nd and 3rd September.**

Left: **One of the information boards proves interesting to one young enthusiast walking the bridge.**

thousands of daily commuters who had watched the bridge being built since 2011 finally got their chance to see for themselves what an improvement the new bridge represents over its predecessor.

As was to be expected, the usual traffic levels were augmented by many thousands of extra vehicles carrying people anxious to be able to say they had crossed the bridge on its very first day of operation. This inevitably led to higher levels of peak hour traffic volume. This was history repeating itself: throughout the six year build programme, members of the construction team had often been pleased to meet people who claimed to have crossed

the Forth Road Bridge on its very first day of operation in 1964 and who were determined to repeat the experience in 2017. Bridges have this effect on people.

For the first few weeks, traffic management regulations were in place to limit traffic to 40mph. Following this initial familiarisation period, full motorway status was introduced and vehicles were allowed to pass over the bridge at 70mph.

Between 1st and 7th September, the bridge was once again closed to traffic to allow not only for the Royal Opening ceremony on the 4th, but to allow tens of thousands of people to walk across the bridge during the weekend of the 2nd and 3rd. A public ballot had been launched by Transport Scotland in June through which members of the public could apply for tickets to take part in the 'Queensferry Crossing Experience'. With the new bridge enjoying motorway status and, therefore, no access for pedestrians, it was to be expected that the ballot for this once-in-a-lifetime opportunity would be over-subscribed. In the event, almost 230,000 applications were received for the 50,000 tickets available.

Above: **Many people walking across the bridge as part of the 'Queensferry Crossing Experience' were raising money for charity.**

Right: **The Commemorative Brochure which was produced for the Official Opening Ceremony.**

A fleet of double-decker buses transferred the lucky ticket holders, many raising money for charity, to and from dedicated park 'n ride facilities on both sides of the Forth. Queensferry Crossing "ambassadors" were on hand to answer any questions about the design and construction of the bridge and information boards along the length of the north and southbound carriageways provided further interesting facts and figures for the walkers as they passed by. The happy and excited 'street party' atmosphere was a fitting welcome from the people to this latest spectacular addition to the country's built heritage.

Finally, on the day after the Royal Opening and as a 'thank you' gesture from the Project team, over 9,500 local people from communities on either side of the Firth of Forth were invited to take part in a 'Queensferry Crossing Day Out' by walking out on to the bridge. This included 6,500 pupils from 13 local schools, reflecting the great interest shown by school children ever since construction work began in 2011.

Taken together, these celebrations formed a fitting culmination to the many years of dedicated and skilful effort put in by so many people to turn the original vision for a new Forth crossing into glorious reality. The Queensferry Crossing now takes its rightful place alongside its two illustrious neighbours, secure in the knowledge that it instils just the same high and enduring degrees of pride, inspiration and affection amongst the people of the country who have firmly taken this 21st century icon of civil engineering to their hearts.

The Queensferry Crossing is launched in a blaze of light.

For a couple of days, the Queensferry Crossing became the largest footbridge in the world with 50,000 people taking advantage of a once-in-a-lifetime opportunity to walk over the bridge.

Opposite page top: **The Queen and Duke of Edinburgh are met by the Lord Lieutenant of Fife, Robert Balfour, on arrival on the north shore.**

Opposite page below: **300 local school pupils were on hand to greet the Queen as she arrived to open the bridge.**

Above: **The Queen cuts the ribbon and declares the bridge officially open.**

Left: **In her speech, the Queen said the three Forth bridges were all feats of modern engineering and paid tribute to the talents, vision and remarkable skills of those who designed and built them.**

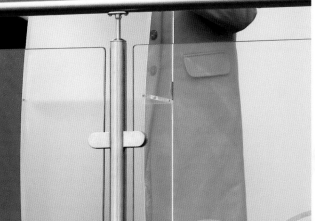

Top: The Queen unveils the plaque watched by the First Minister.

Right: The Royal Bentley takes the Queen and Duke of Edinburgh over the Bridge.

Above: The Queen is presented with a silver model of the Queensferry Crossing by Keith Brown MSP, Cabinet Secretary for Economy, Jobs and Fair Work.

Below: The moment traffic started to flow across the bridge at 1-30am on Wednesday 30th August 2017.

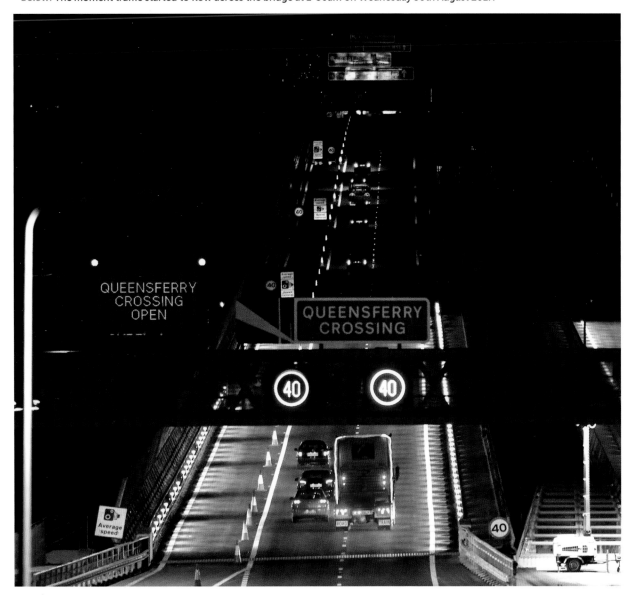

"Queensferry Crossing"
by Jackie Kay, the Scots Makar

If you were a ship you would sail and be gone
but you are the bridge that will stay

You are the ship that does not leave,
that breathes in the sky, night and day

Queensferry Crossing

If your fitters and your welders, your joiners and engineers
Surveyors, scaffolders, concrete finishers and crane
operators

Across Scotland had a dream o' ye -
it would be to see you on this opening day,

Queensferry Crossing

Raising your harp and playing your strings
at every return, every going away,

Back and forth, Firth of Forth
North to South, South to North

Queensferry Crossing

Like a great cormorant, perfectly still,
and lifting your wings out to dry,

in snell winds or high,
come driving rain, come shine,

Queensferry Crossing

You glint, you glimmer, are ne'er the same twice
Your cables shimmer, disappear in the chittering light

Mystery crossing, here one minute, gone another,
In dreich mist, in the haar, in twilight,

Queensferry Crossing

Along St Margaret's marsh, where the pilgrims once were
ferried,
by the banks of the Forth

across time's estuaries, life's vagaries,
its ups and downs – here you are, arms outstretched

Queensferry Crossing

Three bridges; three centuries; one life.
Be shielded, be sheltered, be brave, be kind!

A girl crosses the old red in a crimson dress,
An old man walks the suspension;

Queensferry Crossing

Cars of all colours will drive across the Queensferry
Like the Queen's car did today.

The urge to build bridges runs deeper
than the great rivers they ford

Queensferry Crossing

You're the bridge in the sky, the high hope,
You're the wingspan of centuries, the future's story.

If you were a ship you would sail and be gone
But you are the bridge that will stay.

You are the ship that does not leave
That breathes in the sky night and day

Queensferry Crossing

Queensferry Crossing

Queensferry Crossing

Above: A happy omen, the Northern Lights put on a fine display over the Firth of Forth the day after the Queensferry Crossing was officially opened by Her Majesty The Queen.

Queensferry Crossing Subcontractors and Suppliers

1st Access Rentals Ltd
20/20 Business Insight Ltd
4s Talking Torque Ltd
4U Resourcing Group Ltd
A & K Health & Safety
A & N Management Ltd
A G Brown Fabrications Ltd
A M Fire & Security Systems Ltd
A. Baars Azn Exploitatie
A.J. McAlpine Construction Ltd
A.L. Gordon Engineering Ltd
A.S.A.P. Supplies Ltd
AA Environmental LLP
AB2000 Ltd
Abacus Lighting Ltd
Abba Sealants Ltd
Aberdeen Foundries
ABL Realisations Ltd
Abnormal Load Engineering Ltd
ABS Europe Ltd
ABS Marine Services Ltd
Access Lifting Pulling & Safety Ltd
Access Plus (Scotland) Ltd
Accomplished Personnel
Ace Controls International
ACE INA Services UK Ltd
Aconex Services Ltd
Acorn Signs Ltd
Acoustic1 Ltd
Acre Resources Ltd
Adam Millar & Sons Ltd
Adam Rosolowski Twojebiur UK
Adekson Ltd
Advance Engineering Services
Advanced Resource Managers
Aecom Ltd
Aeropair Ltd
AF Realisations Ltd
AFI-Uplift Ltd
AGD Equipment Ltd
Aggregate Industries UK Ltd
Aggreko UK Ltd
Ainscough Crane Hire Ltd
Ainscough Training Services Ltd

Air Monitors Ltd
Air Products Plc
Air Quality Monitors Ltd
AJ Engineering & Construction
Akdeniz Gemi Insa San. Ve Tic. A.S
Aktien-Gesellschaft der Dillinger
Alan E Wilson
Alan Motion Tree Consulting Ltd
Alan White Design Ltd
Alastair James Maclean
Albion Drilling Group Ltd
Aleph Consultores S.L.P.
Alexander (Scotland) & Co Ltd
Alimak Hek Ltd
Alison Graham
Allianz Engineering Inspection
Allison Enterprises Ltd
AllStar Business Solutions Ltd
Alltec Construction Ltd
Almet Doors Ltd
Alnmaritec Ltd
Alpha Chemicals Ltd
Alpha Translating & Interpreting
alta4 Geoinformatik AG
Altrad Beaver 84 Ltd
American Bridge / Fluor Enterprise
American Bridge International
Amey Highways Ltd
Amphorea Packaging Ltd
Amtech Group Ltd
Anchor Magnets Ltd
Anchor Systems (Europe) Ltd
Ancon Ltd
Anderson Builders Ltd
Andrews Fasteners Ltd
Andrews Sykes Hire Ltd
Angle Park Sand & Gravel Co. Ltd
Anixter Ltd
Anna Henly Photography
Annick Construction Ltd
Annick Structures Ltd
Apex Developments Ltd
Apex Generators Ltd
Apex Industrial Chemicals Ltd

Apogee Corporation Ltd
Applications in Cadd Ltd
Applus RTD UK Ltd
APS Haulage Ltd
Aquamarine Crewing Ltd
Arbuckle Contractors
Arc Site Services Ltd
Arc Steel Commercial Ltd
ArcelorMittal Commercial
Arco Ltd
Armadillo Noise & Vibration Ltd
Arrow Supplies, Nilfisk Ltd
Arthur J. Gallagher (UK) Ltd
ASC Factors Ltd, T/A Arcman
Ashtead Plant Hire Company Ltd
Aspect Land & Hydrographic
Ast Language Services Ltd
ATI Tank Hire Ltd
Atkins Ltd
ATLAS
Atom Consultants (Edinburgh) Ltd
ATP Instrumentation Ltd
ATS Euromaster Ltd
ATV Services Scotland Ltd
Autodesk Development S.a.r.l.
Autodiagnostik (Fife) Ltd
Autodiagnostik Ltd
Automatic Data Processing Ltd
Autotechnik Ltd
Avian Communications Ltd
Avra Towage BV
AXA ICAS Ltd
Axair Fans Uk Ltd
Axiom N D T Ltd
Babcock Marine Ltd
Back Up Partner AB
Balfour Beatty Ground
Banagher Precast Concrete Ltd
Banner Group Ltd
Barbour European Ltd
Barclay & Mathieson Ltd
BASF plc
Batt Cables Ltd
Bay Travel Coaches Ltd

Bayview Carpet Centre
BBC Chartering Carriers
BCS Group
Beamer Rock Excavation JV
Becker Surveys Malcolm Hughes Ltd
Bell Surveys Ltd
Belzona Polymerics Ltd
Bentley Systems International Ltd
Bernard Hunter Ltd
Better Buffets Ltd
Bewehrungsnachweis & Analyse
Bilfinger Construction UK Ltd
Bill Boley Ltd
Billy Bowie Special Projects Ltd
Binn Skips Ltd
Birketts Fencing Ltd
Bits & PC'S (TS) Ltd
Black Light Ltd
Blackwood Plant Hire Ltd
Blairston Cost Management Ltd
Blasting Services Ltd
Blok N Mesh UK Ltd
BLP Cherbourg
Blue Crown Management Ltd
Blue V. Marine Electronics
BOC Ltd
Bogser AB Sven
Bohnenstingl GmbH
Border Barrier Systems Ltd
Borehole Logging Solutions Ltd
Boskalis Offshore Marine
BPH Equipment Ltd
Braisby Roofing Ltd
Brand Energy & Infrastructure
Brauer Ltd
BRC Ltd
BRE Ltd
Brechin Tindal Oatts
Breedon Aggregates Scotland Ltd
Bremicker Verkehrstechnik GmbH
Brian Sutherland Flip Photography
Bridon International Ltd
Briggs Amasco Ltd
Briggs Marine Contractors Ltd
Brimmond Group
British Gas Trading Ltd
British Red Cross Society
British Standards Institution
British Telecommunications Plc
Britpave Barrier Systems Ltd
Brogan Fuels (GB Oils Ltd)
Brooke Edgley Specialist
Brooks MacGregor Ltd

Brookson (5233P) Ltd
Bryceland Total Timber
BSI Assurance UK Ltd
Buckhurst Plant Hire Ltd
Buildbase - Grafton Merchanti
Built Environment Support
Bullions Ltd
Burdens Ltd (WTB Group Ltd)
Bureau Veritas S.A.
Butyl Products Ltd
C & L Tool Distributors, LLC
C Toole Safety Engineering
C&V Carmichael Ltd
C. Brumpton Inspection Ltd
CAD Media UK
Cadzow Heavy Haulage Ltd
Café Giacomo
Caldive Ltd
Caledonia Fire and Security Ltd
Caledonian Laboratories Ltd
Caledonian Petroleum Services Ltd
Calmore Machinery Co Ltd
Calor Gas Ltd
Caltrop Corporation
Calypso Marine Ltd
Camel Concrete Ltd
Camscaff Ltd
Cannon Hygiene (OCS Group)
Cantilever Pty. Ltd
Capita IT Services Ltd
Capital Safety Group
Capital Testing Services Ltd
Capo Projects Group, LLC
Carbonsave Solutions Ltd
Cardiac Science Holdings (UK) Ltd
Carillion Construction Ltd
Carlos Fernandez Casado, S.L.
Carnegie Enterprise Ltd
Carolyn Barton
Carpas Keops SL
Carpenter & Paterson Ltd
Castellan Group Ltd
Castle Group Scotland Ltd
Castle Water Ltd
CBS Selection Ltd
CCC Solutions
CCL Components Ltd
CCS Media
CDI AndersElite Ltd
CDM Consult GmbH
Ceequal Ltd
Celtest Co. Ltd
Cementation Skanska Ltd

Central Calibration Services
Central Concrete Pumping Ltd
Central Training Services Ltd
Centrica plc
Certex Lifting Ltd
CET Structures Ltd
CETCO Europe Ltd
C-FAB Engineering
Chambers Oceanics Ltd
Check-It Scaffold Services Ltd
Chemcem Scotland Ltd
Chemtest Ltd
Cherbourg Terminal Vrac SAS
CHG Safety Ltd
China Railway Baoji Bridge
Chris Powell Consultancy Ltd
Chrystal & Hill Ltd
Cie Cherbourgeoise de Remorquage
City Hotels (Dunfermline) Ltd
City of Bath College
City of Edinburgh Council
City Of Glasgow College
Civils & Drainage Supplies Ltd
CJR Propulsion Ltd
Clan House of Edinburgh Ltd
Class One Traffic Management Ltd
Clee Hill Plant Ltd
Cleveland Bridge UK Ltd
Climatic Services Ltd
CLOB
Cloud Cover IT Services Ltd
Clow Group Ltd
CLR Plant Hire Ltd
Clyde Marine Services Ltd
Clyde Security Containers Ltd
Clyde Travel Ltd
Clydeview Engineering Ltd
Cm Steel Buildings & Concrete
CNG Management International Ltd
Coastal Marine Eyemouth Ltd
Coastway Ltd
Coastworks Operations Ltd
Cofra Ltd
Colcrete - von Essen GmbH & Co. KG
COLINS TYRES
Colle Sittard Machinehandel B.V.
Collett & Sons Ltd
Collier Haulage Ltd
Collier Quarrying & Recycling Ltd
Combisafe International Ltd
Command Alkon Ltd
Commercial Fire Protection Ltd
Communisis UK Ltd

Commutaports Ltd
Compass Contract Services UK Ltd
Competence Matters Ltd
Complete Plastics Solutions Ltd
Complete Stainless Ltd
ComputerLand UK Ltd
Con Forms Europe
Concrete Repairs Ltd
Conquip Engineering Group
Considerate Constructors Scheme Ltd
Conspare Holdings Ltd
ConSpare Ltd
Construction & Property
Construction Fixing Systems Ltd
Construction Industry Publications
Contract Scotland Ltd
Controls Testing
Cooltemple Construction
Cooper and Turner Distribution Ltd
Core Cut Ltd
Core Plant Hire Ltd
Cost Effective Catering Ltd
Coyle Personnel Plc
CPA (Scotland) Ltd
Crane Rail Installations (UK) Ltd
Cranesafe Ltd
Creafix Graphics
Crist S.A.
Crofab Engineering Ltd
Croft Construction Services Ltd
Cromwell Tools Ltd
Crummock (Scotland) Ltd
Cuatrecasas, Goncalves Pereira, S.
Cummins Ltd
Cupar Bearings & Transmissions Ltd
Cuthbertson Laird Instruments Ltd
D & K Welding Services Ltd
D&M Haulage (Mixer Hire) Ltd
D&R Tyres Ltd
D. Brash & Sons Ltd
D. C. Plant Service & Sales Ltd
D. Copeland Engineering Ltd
D. Gibson
D.R. Millar
D`Suza Recruitment Ltd
Dalby Offshore Services Ltd
Dallas & McMillan
Daltons Demolitions Ltd
Danish Technologial Institute
Dann Ltd
Datum Monitoring Services Ltd
David John Smallman
David Kyle t/a D & M Haulage

David Petrie
Davidson & Robertson Ltd
Davidson and McLeish
Dawson Construction Plant Ltd
D-Celtech UK
DCN Diving B.V.
Deanston Cooper Ltd
Deborah Services Ltd
Dee-Organ (Signature Ltd)
Deloitte LLP
Delta Marine Ltd
Delta Rubber Ltd
Deltabloc UK Ltd
Dem-Master Demolition Ltd
Denholm Wilhelmsen Ltd
Denny Plant Hire Ltd
Denny Tipper Transport Ltd
Derek Chambers
Derwent Weighing Ltd
Desk Top Publishing
Develop Training Ltd
Developers Direct Ltd
DFDS Seaways PLC
Dieseko Group B.V.
Dieselec Thistle Generators Ltd
Digital Angel Radio
Dingbro Ltd
Dipl.-Ing. Herwig GmbH
Direct Chemicals Ltd
Dixon Group Europe Ltd
DL Industrial Supplies Ltd
DLA Piper UK LLP
DM Hall LLP
DMJ Inspection Services Ltd
DMS Civils Ltd
DNA Contract Flooring Ltd
DNV GL SE
Doig and Smith Ltd
Doka UK Formwork Technologies Ltd
Dollard Structures Ltd
Dominic Fischer
Donyal Engineering Ltd
Doosan Power Systems Ltd
Dorman Long Technology Ltd
Dovetail Scotland
Dragados S.A.
Drew Graham Contracting Ltd
Drumclog Plant Ltd
Drummond Motor Company Ltd
DSuza Ltd
Dumyat Apartment
Dun & Bradstreet Ltd
Dunfermline VE Ltd

Dunsmore Consultancy Ltd
Dustcontrol UK Ltd
DWF LLP
Dx Recruitment Ltd
Dynatest UK Ltd
Dywidag-Systems International GmbH
E & C Engineering (Yorkshire) Ltd
E & J Douglas & Sons Ltd
E&C Crane Engineering Ltd
E.S.L. (GB) Ltd
Eadon Consulting Ltd
Eastern Vulcanising Services Ltd
EC Services
Ecco Finishing Supplies Ltd
ECoW Solutions Ltd
Eden Springs UK Ltd
EDF Energy Customer Field Services
Edgar Health and Safety Ltd
Edinburgh Leisure
Edmiston Brown & Co Ltd
Edmundson Electrical Ltd
EEG Utilities Ltd
EFCO UK Ltd
Efinor (Normetal)
Ekspan Ltd
Elcometer Ltd
Eldapoint Ltd
Electromech Industrial Ltd
Electronic Temperature Instruments
Elevator Equipment Ltd
Elior UK Ltd
Elite Precast Concrete Ltd
Elliot International (Pty) Ltd
Elliott Group Ltd
EMJ Plastics Ltd
Emperor Design Consultants Ltd
Environmental Reclamation
Environmental Scientifics Group Lt
Envisage Wildcare Ltd
Enzo South West Ltd
Eplass GmbH
Esri (UK) Ltd
ESS Electrical Contractors Ltd
Esteyco SAP
Eti Engineering Ltd
ETLG Ltd
Euro Drive Systems Ltd
Eurojet (Scotland) Ltd
European Metal Recycling Ltd
Evonik Industries AG
Evonik Performance Materials GmbH
EWI Global Ltd
Exova (UK) Ltd

6-30am: one of FCBC's crew boats arrives at the Central Tower at the beginning of another day building the Queensferry Crossing.

Eyemouth Harbour Trust
Fabreeka GB, Inc
FAL Scottish Propeller Service Ltd
Falcon Electrical Engineering Ltd
Falcon Tower Crane Services Ltd
Fastnet Shipping Ltd
Faxco Maintenance Ltd
FBM Contracts Ltd
FenderCare Ltd
Feralco (UK) Ltd
Ferjovi, S.A.U.
Ferrier Pumps Ltd
FES Ltd
Fettes & Rankine
FFEC Ltd
Fieldwork Contracts Ltd
Fife College
Fife Constabulary
Fife Council
Finning (UK) Ltd
FIP Industriale SpA
Fire Risk Assessment Scotland
Firmes Ecologicos Soltec S.A.
First Safety Scotland Ltd
Firwood Timber & Plywood Co. Ltd
Fish Guidance Systems Ltd
FitzGerald Consulting Ltd
Fixing Centre Ltd
Fleet Factors Ltd
Flogas Britain Ltd
Fluorocarbon Ltd
Force Dredging Systems U.K. Limite
Forde Training Services Ltd
Formenti Orlando S.r.l.
Form-Fab (Worcester) Ltd
Forster Industrial Solutions Ltd
Forte Maritime Ltd
Fortel Services Ltd
Forth Design Joint Venture I/S
Forth Logistics Marine Services
Forth Ports Ltd
Forth Power Marine Training
Forth Valley College
Foster Contracting Ltd
Fowler & Holden Ltd
Frazer (Jewson Ltd)
Frontier Pitts Ltd
FTI Consulting LLP
Fugro GB Marine Ltd
Ful-Ton Forklifts Ltd
Fyns Kran Udstyr A/S
G J Reid Quantum Ltd
G P Owen Ltd

G&M Radiator Manufacturing Co. Ltd
G.G.R. Group Ltd
G2 Metric Ltd
G4S Secure Solutions (UK) Ltd
GAC Shipping (UK) Ltd
Gallacher Services Ltd
Galliford Try Plant Ltd
Galt Transport Ltd
Galt Transport Ltd
GAP Group Ltd
Gardiner & Theobald Fairway Ltd
Gardomarc Site Services Ltd
Gareloch Support Services B.V.
Garlock Pipeline Technologies Ltd
GB Geotechnics Ltd
GBS Building Services Ltd
GBS Surface Preparation Ltd
Geckotech Solutions Ltd
Geesepool Communications
Generation Hire & Sale
GEO Laboratory Testing Services Ltd
GEO Site & Testing Services Ltd
Geocentrix Ltd
Geocisa UK Ltd
Geofabrics Ltd
GEO-INFO Ltd
George A Walker Ltd
George Beattie & Sons Ltd
Geosolve
Geotechnical Instruments UK Ltd
Geotechnical Observations Ltd
Geotecnia Y CimientosIMIENTOS S.A.
Geoterra Ltd
German Language Centre
Getmie Safe Ltd
Geyer Plant Services Ltd
GH Planning Ltd
Gibb & Beveridge
Giles Engineering (UK) Ltd
Giro Engineering Ltd
GJC Contracts Ltd
Glasgow Kelvin College
Glasgow Maritime Academy LLP
Glassfibre Flagpoles Ltd
Glenalmond Trading Investments Ltd
Global Navigation Solutions Ltd
Global Project (Services) Ltd
Global Quantum Infrastructure Ltd
Glover Site Investigations Ltd
Glowacki Engineering
GM Utility Services Ltd
Go Plant Ltd
Godfrey Welding Engineering Ltd

Golden Lion Pilotage & Marine
Goldhofer Aktiengesellschaft
GOMACO International Ltd
Gordon Bathgate
Gordon Bow Plant Hire Ltd
Gordon Hollywood Associates Ltd
GP Plantscape Ltd
GPS Marine Contractors Ltd
GPS Sprayers Ltd
Grafton Merchanting GB Ltd t/a PDM
Grahame CM Duff
Grahams The Family Dairy Ltd
Grant Construction Services
Grant Taylor Innovations Ltd
Gray Fabrication Ltd
Gray Forklift Services Ltd
Green Resourcing Ltd
Green Warehouse Ltd
Greenham (Bunzl UK Ltd)
Greenwell Equipment Ltd
Greenwell Equipment Ltd
Greenwood Hire Ltd
Greisinger-Electronic GmbH
Griffiths & Armour
Groeneveld UK Ltd
Grommets Ltd
Grontmij Ltd
Groutation Ltd
Grupo SYO Estructuras S.L.
Grupo Tecade S.L.
GSI Events Ltd
GS-Hydro UK Ltd
G-TEC, Business Energy Ltd
GTG Training Ltd
Guangzhou Webforge Grating Ltd
Günter Harring
Gurney Slade Lime & Stone Co. Ltd
Guyspen Associates
GW Hire Ltd
H&F Drilling Supplies Ltd
H&MV Engineering Ltd
H.E.S. SALES Ltd
Halcrow Group Ltd
Halyard (M & I) Ltd
Hamilton & Inches Ltd
Hammelmann Maschinenfabrik GmbH
Hammond Concrete
Hanson Quarry Products Europe Ltd
Harbour HR Ltd
Hardstaff Traffic Barrier
Harris Steel Services Ltd
Harsco Infrastructure Services
Haulotte UK Ltd

Hayward Associates
Hazco Environmental Ltd
Hazlett Metals Ltd
HB Tunnelling Ltd
HBPW LLP
HE Hans Eibinger Mo. Kft.
Headland Archaeology (UK) Ltd
Health and Safety Executive
Hebetec Engineering AG
Helirig Ltd
Helix Safety Ltd
Henry Gillies Contractors Ltd
Herbert Smith Freehills LLP
Hessle Plant Ltd
Hewden Stuart Ltd
Hewson Consulting Engineers Ltd
Hexagon Metrology Ltd
Highland Fuels Ltd
Highland Industrial Supplies Ltd
High-Point Rendel Ltd
Highsparks TCS Ltd
Hill & Smith Ltd
Hill International (UK) Ltd
Hilman Rollers International Inc
Hilti GB Ltd
Hire Station Ltd
HKA Global Ltd
HL Plant Ltd
Hochtief (UK) Construction Ltd
Hodge Clemco Ltd
Hoelscher Wasserbau GmbH
Hoist Sales Uk Ltd
HoleMaker Technology Ltd
Holemasters Scotland Ltd
Holmstrom Inspection Ltd
Hopetoun Crescent Property Ltd
Hopetoun Estate
Horiba Mira Ltd
Hose Direct Ltd
Hose World Ltd
HSE Scotland Ltd
HTC Fastenings Ltd
HTL Group Ltd
Hudson Global Resources Ltd
Hugh K. Gillies (Construction)
Hughes Offshore Group Ltd
Hunter Demolition (George)
Hydra Capsule Ltd
Hydrainer Pump Hire Ltd
Hydrajaws Ltd
Hymix Ltd
Hypro Developments Ltd
Hy-Tex (UK) Ltd

I & C Ltd
Iain Weir (Supplies) Ltd
IAM Drive & Survive Ltd
Ian R. Hanby
Ian Robertson
IBI Group (Uk) Ltd
IC Consultants Ltd
ICL Tech Ltd
IKM Consulting Ltd
IKM Visual Solutions Ltd
Imes Ltd
Impact Signs
Impact Test Equipment Ltd
Imtech Traffic & Infra Uk Ltd
In Situ Site Investigation Ltd
Indicia Training Ltd
Indutec Umwelttechnik
Innovative Utilities (Uk) Ltd
Insight Training (Scotland) Ltd
In-Situ Europe Ltd
Institute of Risk Management
Institution of Civil Engineers
Instituto Tecnico de Materiales
Interlink M74 JV
International Timber (Saint-Gobain)
Intruder Detection & Electrical
IOM Consulting Ltd
IPH Fulmer
IPP Education Ltd
Irlequip Ltd
Is Instruments Receivables 2014 Ltd
Ischebeck Titan Ltd
Isolearn Education Ltd
IT4Automation Ltd
IVIC Ltd
J & H M Dickson Ltd
J B Management (Scotland) Ltd
J E M Engines Ltd
J. F. MacDonald
J. G. Martin Plant Hire Ltd
J. M. Martin Ltd
J.B. Site Investigations
J.P. Whelan & Sons
J.S. Pneumatic
Jade-Dienst GmbH
James Blake & Co (Engineers) Ltd
James Cowie & Co. Ltd
James Harbison & Company
James Jones & Sons Ltd
James Penman Plant Hire Ltd
Jan Prentice HSE & Training Services
Janson Bridging (UK) Ltd
Jarvie Plant Ltd

JC Drilling
JC Peacock and Company Ltd
JC. Gillespie (Engineering) Ltd
JCK Translation
Jewers Doors Ltd
JKS Boyles UK Ltd
JMS Lincoln Ltd
Joaquin Pereira Mata
Joe Roocroft & Sons Ltd
John Davidson (Pipes) Ltd
John Hudson Trailers Ltd
John Lawrie (Aberdeen) Ltd
John McNicol & Co.
John Meiklem Drainage
John Shepherd Boat Transport
John Smith & Son Group Ltd
John Tracey Welding Ltd
John Williamson
John Williamson Electrical Ltd
John Wilson Plant
Jonathan Smith ADI
JP Camera Repair Co
JP Knight (Caledonian) Ltd
JP O'Hare
JR Technical Services UK Ltd
Jungheinrich UK Ltd
K & I LTD
Kapital Assets Ltd
Keep Right Traffic
Keighley Laboratories Ltd
Keith A Umpleby Ltd
Kelly´s Hero Charters
Key Industrial Equipment Ltd
Keyline Builders Merchants Ltd
Keynetix Ltd
Kier Mg Ltd
Kier Plant Ltd
Kimberly Rentals Group Ltd
Klaus H. Ostenfeld
Klohn Crippen Berger Ltd
KN Environmental Services Ltd
Kongsberg Geoacoustics Ltd
Kotug International B.V.
KSG Acoustics Ltd
L & S Engineers Ltd
L.C. Technical Services
Land & Mineral Survey Services Ltd
Landfall Marine Contractors B. V.
Langstane Press Ltd
Lansford Access Ltd
LARSA, Inc.
Laser Stonecleaning Ltd
Latest Technology Ltd (Datascope)

Lavendon Access Services (UK) Ltd
LBD Creative Ltd
LD Associates Training Services
Lee Brothers Bilston Ltd
Leengate Industrial & Welding
Leith and Granton Boatmen
Level Developments Ltd
LGAI Technological Center, S.A.
Liebherr Great Britain Ltd
Lifting & Marine Services Ltd
Lifting Gear Uk (Asset Management)
Link projekt s.r.o.
Lily Publications Ltd
Lloyds British Testing Ltd
Lloyds Register EMEA
Lloyds Register Quality Assurance
Load Systems UK Ltd
LOC Hire Ltd
Lomond Electrical Ltd
Lomond Plant Ltd
London Offshore Consultants Ltd
Loxam Access Ltd
M & S Engineering Ltd
M J Hughes Ltd
Mabey Bridge Ltd
Mabey Hire Ltd
Mac Plant Services Ltd
Maccaferri Ltd
Macdonald Houstoun House Hotel
MacGregor Industrial Supplies Ltd
Maclean and Speirs Blasting Ltd
Macloch Construction Ltd
Madden Contracts Ltd
mageba sa
Magnet Expert Ltd
Maid of the Forth
Mainbrace Marine Ltd
Malcargo Marine Services
Malcolm Hughes
Malin Industrial Concrete Floors Ltd
Malin Marine Consultants Ltd
MAN Truck & Bus UK Ltd
Manuplas Ltd
Marine & Towage Services Group Ltd
Marine Electrical Installations Ltd
Marine Publications
Marine Services Eyemouth Ltd
Mariteam Personnel Services B.V.
Markon Ltd
Martin Barlow Welding & Inspection
Marwood Group Ltd
Masonry Solutions Ltd
Maspero Elevatori S.p.A.

Master-Peace Recruitment Ltd
MATtest Site Services Ltd
Mau Quan International Company Ltd
Maxx Piling Stockholders Ltd
McCalls Special Products Ltd
McCarthy Taylor Systems Ltd
McDonald Scaffolding (Services) Ltd
McEvoy Engineering Ltd
Mcgrattan Piling And Supplies Ltd
Mckenzie Concrete Pumps Ltd
McLean Buchanan & Wilson Lim
McLean Fabrication Solutions Ltd
McMillan Plant Ltd
McMullan Shellfish
McPhee Bros (Blantyre) Ltd
Mekano4 S.A.
Mellicks Solicitors & Notaries
Melvilles Car Wash
Melville's Taxis
Meon LLP
Mercian Weldcraft Ltd
Merkland Tank Ltd
Met Office
Metalurgica Del Guadalquivir, S.L.
MetTech UK
MFV Marine Ltd
MG Construction Ltd
MG Duff International Ltd
MGM Timber (Scotland) Ltd
Michael Lynagh
Michael Owens
Micro Drainage Ltd
Midland Steel Reinforcement
Midland Steel Traders Ltd
Miers Construction Products Ltd
Millar Callaghan Engineering
Millennium Personnel Services Ltd
Miller Fabrications Ltd
Millfield Enterprises
MIL-TEK (Environmental) Ltd
Minelco Ltd
Minerex Geophysics Ltd
Mines Rescue Service Ltd
Misco UK Ltd
Mistras Group Ltd
Mitchell Diesel Ltd
MK Engineering Services Ltd
Mk4 Technical International SL
Molplant Construction Ltd
Moog GmbH Brückenuntersichts
Moristir Ltd
Morrison Construction (Galliford Try Plc)
Morxol Marine Ltd

Mott Macdonald Ltd
Mount Plant
Mr. Stephen Furst QC.
MSBL&P Ltd Ltd
MTS Nationwide Ltd
Mudfords Ltd
Muir Construction Ltd
Mulholland Contracts Ltd
Mulholland Plant Services Ltd
Munro Consulting Group Ltd
Munro Energy and Infrastructure Ltd
Munro Solutions (Scotland) Ltd
Murdoch MacKenzie Construction Ltd
Murform Ltd
Murray Commercial Ltd
Mus Utility Services Ltd
MV Commercial Ltd
MV Trench Support Ltd
MW Groundworks Ltd
National Access and Scaffolding
National Construction College
Nationwide Crash Repair Centres Ltd
NAVIS elektronika
Neopost Ltd
Neptune Marine Service BV
NES Track Ltd
Netek IR System A/S
Netlatch Ltd
New Metals And Chemicals Ltd
New Pig Ltd
Niddry Bing Ltd
NIM Mech Ltd
NIRAS Fraenkel Ltd
Nixon Hire (John Nixon Ltd)
Noble Denton Consultants Ltd
NÖLLE Industrielle
Normand & Thomson (Hillend) Ltd
North East Yacht Surveys
Northburn Oils Ltd
Northcliff Holiday
Northern Survey Supplies Ltd
Novatech Measurements Ltd
Npower Ltd
NRL Ltd
NWH Construction Services Ltd
Nylacast Ltd
Occupational Health Works Ltd
Ocean Engineering (Fire) Ltd
Ocean Safety Ltd
Ocean Science Consulting Ltd
Oceaneering International
Ofcom Office of Communications
Office Angels Ltd

Ogilvie Fleet Ltd
Onsite Hire Ltd
Onsite MSP Ltd
op5 AB
Optimum MBA Ltd
Oracle Corporation UK Ltd
Orbital Fasteners Ltd
Osprey Concrete Structures Ltd
Osprey Shipping Ltd
Outreach Ltd
Outsourced Design & Construction
P & H Civils Ltd
P. F. La Roche & Company Ltd
P. R. Gaunt Technical
PACT Enterprises Ltd
Page Personnel
Paragon Group UK Ltd SP
Paragon Power Services Ltd
Parker Merchanting
Paul Edgar t/a Edgar Health
PC Plant & Partners Ltd i.L.
PDC Plant Ltd
Peace Recruitment
Pegasus Power & Communications Ltd
Pentland Locksmiths Services
Pepcon Ltd
PERI Ltd
Perryman´s Buses Ltd
PES (UK) Ltd
Peter H. J. Chapman
Peter Madsen Rederi A/S
Peter Stevenson Consultants Ltd
Petrofac Training Ltd
Pfeifer Drako Ltd
PFJ Safety Ltd
Phil Bamforth Consulting Ltd
PHL Sales Ltd
Phoenix Specialist Solutions Ltd
PHU JAD S.C.
Pickerings Europe Ltd
Pile Breaking Systems (UK) Ltd
Pinsent Masons LLP
Pipeco Europe Ltd
Pipeline & Drainage Systems Ltd
Pipemore (Scotland) Ltd
Pipeshield International Ltd
Pirtek (George Colliar Ltd)
Pitcairn Engineering Ltd
Pitchmastic Pmb Ltd
Planet Ocean Ltd
Plant Glazing Ltd
Plant Handling Ltd
Plantfinder (Scotland) Ltd

Plastic Solutions (Aldridge) Ltd
Plastics W. Graham Ltd
Platipus Anchors Ltd
Pointer Ltd
Polybags Ltd
Pontoon Hire Ltd
Porr Bau GmbH
Port de Cherbourg SAS
Port Edgar Marina Ltd
Portable & Modular Services Ltd
Power Tool Engineering Ltd
Powerflow Solutions Ltd
Powerjet Rentals Ltd
Premier Windscreens
Princess Management Ltd
Principia Ingenieros Consultores SA
Printing Services (Scotland) Ltd
Prodrive Solutions Ltd
Prof. Schiffers Bauconsult
Professional Concrete
Progress Plant (Yorkshire) Ltd
Project Dewatering Ltd
Prolek Auto Electrical Services Ltd
Proserve Ltd
Proteus Equipment Ltd
Provincial Floors Ltd
Proyectos Navales Del Sur S.L.
Pulse Surveying Ltd
Pump Parts Ltd
Putzmeister Concrete Pumps GmbH
Putzmeister Ltd
Pyeroy Group Ltd
QMI Scotland Ltd
Qualsafe Ltd
Quantum International Consulting Ltd
Quartz Scientific Computing Ltd
Quay Diving Services Ltd
QuayQuip B.V.
Queensferry Hotel
Queensferry Life
Quimica Industrial Mediterranea SL
R & G Williams (Ruthin) Ltd
R3 Data Recovery Ltd
R3 Polygon UK Ltd
Radman Associates Ltd
Ramboll UK Ltd
Ramsay & Sons (Forfar) Ltd
Randolph Transport Ltd
Randstad CPE Ltd
Rapid Fire Services Ltd
Ravestein Container Pontoon B.V.
Raymond Goulding
RDL Welding Inspections Ltd

Reactec Ltd
Readman Steel Ltd
Recycling and Data Service Ltd
Red7Marine Ltd
Reekie Machine (Sales) Ltd
Reel Ltd
Regal Rubber Partnership LLP
Regency Doors & Stairs
Regent Office Care Ltd
Reilly Concrete Pumping Ltd
Rentokil Pest Control
RG Model Services Ltd
RHC Lifting Ltd
Ribble Enviro Ltd
Richard Irvin Energy Solutions
Richard Murray Plant Hire
RICS
Righton Ltd
Rigmar Services Ltd
Rimec Ltd
Rippin Ltd
Ritchey Ltd
RJM Ground Solutions Ltd
RMD Kwikform Ltd
RNP Associates Ltd
Robert Hopkins
Robert Peebles
Robert Purvis Plant Hire Ltd
Robert Russel Crow
Robert Wilson
Robust Boats Ltd
Rod Stein Video
Rodio GmbH Spezialtiefbau
Rollo Engineering Ltd
Romtech Ltd
Rondean
Roofing Insulation Services Ltd
Rope & Sling Specialists Ltd
Ropelink Ltd
RoSPA Enterprises Ltd
Ross Electrical
Rotrex Winches
Royal Mail Group Ltd
Royston Ltd
RS Hydro Ltd
RS Machinery
RS Safety Services Ltd
RSM Hire Ltd
RSM UK Tax and Accounting Ltd
RT Claire Ltd (LLC)
Rublane Ltd t/a Lothian
Russell & Ruffino SL
Ryan Civils Ltd

Ryder Services Ltd
S & D Employment Services Ltd
S.W. Directional Drilling Ltd
SAC Commercial Ltd
Saferoad UK Ltd
Safetek Systems Ltd
Safety Check Engineering Ltd
Safety First (Scotland) Ltd
Safety Kleen UK Ltd
Safety, Welding & Lifting
Saint-Gobain Construction
Sale Associates Ltd
Saltire Hospitality Ltd
Sandberg LLP
Sarens UK Ltd
Sarum Hardwood Structures Ltd
Savoir Faire & Cie
Scarborough Muir Group Ltd
SCCS Survey Equipment Ltd
Scheuerle Fahrzeugfabrik GmbH
Schwing Stetter (UK) Ltd
Scientific Analysis
SCMS
Scot Industrial Air
Scot JCB Ltd
ScotAsh Ltd
Scotia Cleanpave
Scotia Handling Services Ltd
Scotimage.com Ltd
Scotline Communications Ltd
Scotsafe Safety Solutions
Scott Direct Ltd
Scottish Agricultural College
Scottish Civils Training Group Ltd
Scottish Water Business
Scottish Water Wholesale
Scottish Power Energy Retail Ltd
SCRL SECO CVBA
Sea And Land Training (Salt)
Seafari Marine Services Ltd
Seaflex Ltd
Seals + Direct Ltd
Search Consultancy Ltd
Securi Group Services Ltd
Security and Fire Equipment
Security-Label.co.uk
SELECT
Select Plant Hire Company Ltd
Selman Marine Design Ltd
Selwood Ltd
SEPA Scottish Environment
Sercal Materials Testing
Service Point UK Ltd

Severn Bore Piling Ltd
Seymour Global Ltd
SGS Engineering UK Ltd
Sgs Mis Testing Ltd
Shanghai Weijing Engineering
Shanghai Zhenhua Heavy
Shaw & Paterson Ltd
Shay Murtagh (Pre-Cast) Ltd
She Software Ltd
Sheet Piling (UK) Ltd
Shepherd Engineering Services Ltd
Ships Electronic Services Ltd
Shirley Parsons Associates Ltd
Shred-it Ltd
Sibbald Ltd
Sibcas Ltd
SIG Trading Ltd
Sign Plus Ltd
Signature Industries Ltd
Siltbuster Ltd
Silver Shield Windscreens Ltd
Simply Rhino Ltd
Sinbad Marine Services Ltd
Siport XXI, S.L.
SIS (Sandy Inspection Services Ltd
Slt Schaudt Industrietechnik
Site Equip Ltd
Site Sealants Ltd
SiteLink Communication Ltd
Skene Group Construction
Skene Group Ltd
Skymasts Antennas Ltd
Sladen Partnership Ltd
SLD Pumps and Power
SMIT Heavy Lift Europe B.V.
SMRU Ltd
Sodak Ltd
Soil Instruments Ltd
Solar Towage Inc.
Somai S.r.l.
Sosia Constructions UK Ltd
Sotra Marine Produkter AS
South Coast Concrete Pumping Ltd
South Staffs (Farms) Ltd
South Tyneside College
Sovereign Steel Ltd
SP Distribution Ltd
Span Access Solutions Ltd
Spanners Mixer Hire Ltd
Spartan Rescue Ltd
Spectrum Metrology Ltd
Speedcrete CP Ltd
Speedy Asset Services Ltd

SPEL Products
SPI Appleton Ltd
Spray Tanker Services Ltd
SQA
SSE Energy Supply Ltd
SSR Ltd
SSP Specialist Surface
Stabilised Pavements Ltd
Stahl CraneSystems Ltd
Stanger Testing Services Ltd
Statfield Tachograph Ltd
Statfield Training Services Ltd
Steel Developments Ltd
Steelfields Ltd
Stefan Steger
Stefanos Gkoutziantamis
Steffens Engineering GmbH
Stewart Paton Associates Ltd
Stewart Plant Sales Ltd
Stewart's Handyman Services
Stirling Lloyd Contracts Ltd
Stirling Lloyd Contruction Ltd
Storie Marine Ltd
Stott Plant Hire Ltd
STR Ltd
Strainstall James Fisher
Strainstall UK Ltd
Strang Recovery Ltd
Streamline Shipping Agencies Ltd
STS Group Ltd
Stuart Group Ltd
Stud Steel S.L.
Sub-Contractor Management Ltd
Süd-Chemie UK Ltd
Suministros Dobra, S.L.
Sundolitt Ltd
Super Rod Ltd
SureScreen Diagnostics Ltd
Survey Connection Scotland Ltd
Survey One Ltd
Survey Solutions Scotland
Survey Supplies Ltd T/A KOREC
Survitec Service & Distribution Ltd
Susiephone Ltd
Svendborg Bugser A/S
Svensk Byggnadsgeodesi AB
SVITZER MARINE LTD
SW Global Resourcing Ltd
Symmons Madge Associates Ltd
Synergie Training Ltd
Syntec Manufacturing Ltd
T & F Handelsonderneming B.V.
T&J Farnell Ltd

Tackle Store Ltd
Taggatach Ltd
Tallix Ltd
Targe Towing Ltd
Tarmac Trading Ltd
Tartanmoose Trading Ltd
Taylor Maxwell & Co. Ltd
Tayside Marine Services Ltd
Tayside Pressure Washers
TCS Chandlery Ltd
TeamFurmanite Ltd
Tech Trader Pro Ltd
Technical Cranes Ltd
Technology Desking Ltd
TECNI Ltd
Tecozam United Kingdom Ltd
Teeside University
Ten 47 Ltd
Tension Control Bolts Ltd
Tensorex Company Inc.
The Art Centre
The Bosuns Locker
The British Abrasives Federation
The British Constructional
The Broadcasting Business Ltd
The Concrete Society Ltd
The Danwood Group Ltd
The Edinburgh Copy Shop Ltd
The Grab Specialist B.V.
The Highfield Recruitment
The Institute of Acoustics Ltd
The Knowledge Academy Ltd
The Lubricant Company Ltd
The Networking Company
The Open University
The Scottish Road
The University of Edinburgh
Thermac (Hire) Ltd
Thermal Hire Ltd
thinkWhere Ltd
Thistle Hydraulics Ltd
Thistle Locks and Alarms Ltd
Thom Micro Systems Ltd
Thomas Graham Transport Ltd
Thomas Gunn
Thomas Muir (Rosyth) Ltd
Thomas Potter (1982) Ltd
Thomas Telford Ltd
Thompson Joint Integrity
Thomson & Partners
Thorco Shipping A/S
Thornbridge Sawmills Ltd

Tides Marine International Ltd
TLM Projects Ltd
T-Mac Construction Ltd
TMS Barrier Services (UK) Ltd
TNT UK Ltd
Tony Beal Ltd
Tony Gee and Partners LLP
TOP CAL Informatica s.l.
Total Concept Logistics Ltd
Total Gas & Power Ltd
TPM Media Planning & Buying Ltd
TPS Weldtech Ltd
Trad Hire & Sales Ltd
Trad Safety Systems Ltd
TRC Companies, Inc.
TREND PROJEKT Sp. z o.o.
Treatment Visual Productions Ltd
Trescal Ltd
Tri-Fix Industrial Fasteners Ltd
TRINAC GmbH
Trinity House Light Dues General
TRL Ltd
Trueform Engineering Ltd
T-Technics B.V.
Tubeclip Ltd
Tufcoat Ltd
Tufnol Composites Ltd
Turner Geotechnical Associates Ltd
Turner Hire Drive Ltd
Turners (Soham) Ltd
Tweed Formwork & Joinery
Twenty Twenty Safety
TWI Ltd
Tyco Fire & Integrated
Tyne Gangway (Structures) Ltd
Tyson's (Ships Riggers) Ltd
UCATT
UK Cables Ltd
UK OPEN IT LTD
UK Sailing Academy (UKSA)
UK Screed & Grout Pumps Ltd
UKAS
UKOS
Unique Events Ltd
United Moulders Ltd
United Plant Service Ltd
Univar Specialty Consumables Ltd
Universal Crane Mats Ltd
Universal Sealants (U.K.) Ltd
University Hospitals Birmingham
University of Derby
University of Dundee

University of Liverpool
University of Salford
University of Strathclyde
Urofoam Ltd
UTE Megusa Tecade Edinburgh
UTEC Geomarine Ltd
Utec Star Net Geomatics Ltd
Utranazz Importers
Vaisala Ltd
Val-U-Blinds Ltd
Van de Wetering
Van Haagen Kraanvouw B.V.
Van Monster (Northgate)
Vantech Engineering Services Ltd
Vaston Ltd
VEGA Environmental Consultants Ltd
Venesky-Brown Recruitment Ltd
Verder Ltd
Vesab Ltd JKS
VFM-FRC Joint Venture Partnership
Vibro Menard Ltd
Vibrock Ltd
Videonations Ltd
Viking Life-Saving Equipment Ltd
Vision Express (UK) Ltd
Vodafone Ltd
Vohkus Ltd
Volker Laser Ltd
VolkerBrooks Ltd
Volvo Group UK Ltd
VP PLC
Vryhof Anchors BV
VSL Systems (UK) Ltd
VTI/Poul Erik Christensen
Vysionics ITS Ltd
W H Malcolm Ltd
W J Electrical Supplies Ltd
Walker Motors Ltd
Walter Watson Ltd
Watkins Hire Ltd
Watson & Hillhouse Ltd
Watson-Towers Ltd
WB Alloy Welding Products Ltd
WEC Group Ltd
Weldex (International) Offshore Ltd
Wemo-Tec UK Ltd
Wernick Hire Ltd
West Of Scotland Storage Ltd
West Track Gateway Ltd
Western Automobile Company Ltd
Western Global Ltd
Westica Communications Ltd

Weston Transport Ltd
WG Tanker Services Ltd
WGM Engineering Ltd
Wheelwash Ltd
White & Co Plc (Forres)
Whiteford Geoservices Ltd
WhiteHouse Studios
Wholesale Welding Supplies Ltd
Whyte Crane Hire Ltd
Wi-Link Solutions Ltd
William Houston
William Johnston & Co
William Tracey Ltd
William Whyte Cargo Handlers Ltd
Willis Ltd
Wilson Contracts Ltd

WindCat Workboats Ltd
Wingate Electrical Plc
Wireless Logic Ltd
Wisa Ltd
WJ Groundwater Ltd
Wm Anderson Engineering Ltd
WM Plant Hire Ltd
Wm. L. COLLIN
Wolseley UK Ltd t/a Burdens
Wolseley UK Ltd
Wolseley Utilities Ltd
Wolters Kluwer (UK) Ltd
Wood Group Industrial
Woodster Realisations Ltd
WWH Construction Ltd
WWM Rose & Sons Ltd

XL Systems Ltd
Xpedite Ltd
Yellow Shield Ltd
Yendall Hunter Ltd
York Survey Supply Centre Ltd
Young Plant & Equipment Sales Ltd
Your Electrical Supplies,
Yuill & Dodds Ltd
ZAGREB-MONTAZA d.o.o. (Ltd)
Zarafa Height Solutions Ltd
Zenith International Freight Ltd
Zenith S.A.S. Ltd
ZPMC
Zurich Insurance plc